Placing Words

Placing Words

Symbols, Space, and the City

William J. Mitchell

The MIT Press
Cambridge, Massachusetts
London, England

MIT Press books may be purchased at special quantity discounts for business or sales promotional use. For information, please email special_sales@mitpress.mit.edu or write to Special Sales Department, The MIT Press, 55 Hayward Street, Cambridge, MA 02142.

This book was set in Stone Sans and Stone Serif by SNP Best-set Typesetter Ltd., Hong Kong and was printed and bound in the United States of America.

Library of Congress Cataloging-in-Publication data

Mitchell, William J. (William John), 1944–
Placing words : symbols, space, and the city / William J. Mitchell.
    p. cm.
Includes index.
ISBN 0-262-63322-1 (pbk. : alk. paper)
1. Communication in architecture. 2. Cities and towns. 3. Public spaces. I. Title.
NA2584.M58 2005   720'.1—dc22   2005049618

10 9 8 7 6 5 4 3 2 1

For Jane

Contents

In the First Place

Shouting "fire" in a crowded theater produces a dramatically different effect from barking the same word to a squad of soldiers with guns. Writing it on a hydrant yields yet another result. The meaning of a message depends not only upon the information that it contains, but also upon the sort of local ignorance or uncertainty that it reduces—in other words, upon what the message's recipients require information *about*. Occupants of a flaming theater need to know that they should make for the exits. Members of a firing squad need to know exactly when to pull the trigger. A fireman facing an array of plumbing fixtures needs to know where to attach the hose. But if I receive the text message FIRE on my mobile phone, at some random moment, I can only respond with a puzzled HUH? Information becomes useful and messages serve their purposes in particular places at particular times. Context matters.

This book explores the ways in which the spaces and places of twenty-first century cities provide contexts for communication—serving not only to shelter and protect their inhabitants, but also to ground and sustain meaningful interaction among them, and to construct community.

Words spoken in place

Sometimes spoken words provide information about physical objects in the immediate vicinity of the conversation. The traffic light is red. Watch out for that car! Please pass the salt. In these cases, speaker and listener share a place and a moment. The directions of their gazes, gestures such as pointing and touching, the effects of walls, stages, desktops, tabletops, frames and other bounding devices, and mere proximity help to pick out, from among all the things in the world, the specific ones that the words are about. The meaning of a local, synchronous, spoken message is a joint product of the words, the body language of the participants in the exchange, and the setting.

Stage and film directors know that, in order to flesh out the meaning of the words provided by a playwright, they must create an appropriate mise-en-scène—a place populated with objects for the words to refer to. (Radio plays, films shot entirely in tight close-up on the faces of the actors, and Samuel Becket in his bare stage mode are instructive limit cases.) Change the set, costumes, and props—by setting *Macbeth* in Washington, say—and the significance of the dialogue will shift. Rewrite the dialogue and it will assign new meaning to the same things. In much the same fashion, by providing tangible, visible referents, the spaces of actual buildings and cities participate in constructing the meaning of the speech that unfolds within them. Reciprocally, spoken sentences like "The meeting is in the second room on the left," and "This was the scene of the crime," add significance to spaces and their contents. As conversations unfold within particular architectural settings, they build up increasingly dense webs of shared understanding grounded—at least in part—on the points of reference that these settings afford.

Furthermore, boundaries of spaces often delimit the scopes of spoken assertions, as in: "Everyone in this room is sworn to secrecy." To understand what the speaker intends, you need to know the relevant spatial limits. When you announce,

"I'm going out," or ask, "May I come in?" you depend upon the clarity of the relevant architectural boundaries to establish precisely what you mean.

When spatial boundaries are ambiguous, or subject to redefinition, you can get conundrums. Within the limits of the world known to Europeans, for example, it was once true to say: "All swans are white." But when the discovery of Australia expanded this world, it also destroyed the truth of the generalization, since Australian swans are black. When Jimi Hendrix sang, "The traffic lights turn blue on Sundays," the boundaries were ambiguous. Maybe the guitar king from Seattle was telling us the truth, but exactly what traffic lights was he talking about? Where? When a Cretan claims, "All Cretans are liars," he creates a notorious paradox, but when a Cretan on vacation in Athens announces, "Everyone back home in Crete is a liar," he may be libeling his countrymen, but there is no logical problem.

Creating the mise-en-scène

The most obvious way to create a mise-en-scène to support communication is to gather objects in a space, such as a room, where they are simultaneously visible, and where not only the objects themselves but also the spatial relationships among them can assume significance. This is the mechanism at work when you collect your private possessions in a container (not only to protect them, but also to assert that they are yours), and when you place valued objects on honorific surfaces such as desktops and mantelpieces while tossing discarded objects into the trash—expecting that the cleaners will read the message correctly. It enables Westminster parliamentarians to define themselves as members of the government or of the opposition by seating themselves on opposite sides of the house. It operates at an architectural scale when centrality asserts the importance of a building or an entrance relative to others, or a corner office suggests the status of its occupant. On your computer screen, it enables the expression of commands not by typing or speaking them, but by dragging icons from window to window, or into the trash.

A second possibility is to arrange objects along a circulation route so that they appear in sequence like successive sentences in a narrative or scenes in a film. Here, patterns of clustering and sequencing can become significant. Paintings in a museum may be hung in chronological order; books on library shelves may be arranged by their Dewey Decimal numbers; and items in a supermarket may be displayed with like items in labeled aisles and sections. Architects may organize spaces along circulation routes to present sequences of views, or to create staged transitions from public to private space, or perhaps from profane to sacred. Theme park rides invert the standard theatrical strategy of presenting successive scenes in the same space to an audience that remains fixed in place, and instead move audiences through scenes that occupy adjacent spaces and play simultaneously.

Like music that gains its effect from both the simultaneity of sounds and the unfolding succession of sounds, then, the interconnected spaces of a city construct a mise-en-scène through both the synchronic effect of simultaneously visible elements and relationships and the diachronic effect of elements and relationships presenting themselves sequentially to moving observers. This dual character of architectural and urban space shows up in strategies for giving directions: you can trace a route to a destination on a map, which shows everything simultaneously, or you can specify a sequence of landmarks and intersections together with turn instructions at each one. A GPS-based automobile navigation system plays it both ways by keeping track of the driver's location in a continuously updated map and providing a sequence of turn instructions in real time.

Of course our movements through buildings and cities, and our opportunities to assemble at various points, are far from unconstrained. In fact, cities operate as huge machines for sorting their populations and organizing opportunities for face-to-face encounter and exchange. Times Square and Trafalgar Square are central, accessible, highly public spaces that attract vast numbers of people, present those people to one another, and offer at least the physical possibility of random meetings—together with its flip side, the possibility of lonely anonymity among the crowds. Sites of commerce—markets, stores, shopping malls, restaurants, bars, bordellos, and airports—occupy somewhat less central locations within the urban fabric, attract more specialized populations, and have more powerful exclusion mechanisms. Churches, mosques, clubs, schools, child-care centers, and courts of law are typically more selective and specialized still—or, at least, differentiated along different dimensions. Private homes place very strong restrictions on co-presence, and boudoirs, teenager bedrooms, dens, and studies within them may be even more restricted—as appropriate to the most private discourse.

Each of these place types provides the necessary boundaries, scenery, and props for the associated characteristic type of spoken discourse. You can say some sorts of things in public and others in private. The language of commerce, the language of the law, the language of liturgy, and the language of intimacy all have their places, while these places set expectations and conventions for the interchanges that unfold within them. Sometimes, as well, the speaker's location confers particular authority, as in speaking from the chair, from the bench, or *ex cathedra*, or imposes particular obligations, as in speaking from the witness box. Knowing what you can say where is a crucial component of effective community membership, while speaking out of place is a challenge to community norms that may get you ostracized or exiled—sent to a place of exclusion.

But the mechanisms described so far merely establish the lowest layers of the city's support for communication. Physical objects and spaces also carry associations and evoke memories. Any thing that you see, hear, smell, or touch may make you think of something else. Any element of the surrounding scene may serve as a link to memories of past events and distant places, to narratives that you have heard, and to facts that you have learned. These linkages may derive from reflexes, as with Pavlov's dogs salivating at the sound of a bell. They may operate through resemblance, visual metaphor, metonymy, or synecdoche. They construct a virtual mise-en-scène on the substructure of the immediate physical one.

The virtual mise-en-scène provides more for you to think about, and to the extent that your companions share it, more for you to talk about. Some buildings, such as cathedrals and monuments, are designed to function primarily as sites of evocation in this way. Some, such as Maya Lin's minimalist Vietnam War Memorial in Washington, have little or no other purpose. In others, such as industrial warehouses, the architecture's evocative qualities may be of distinctly secondary importance, but they are never entirely absent. Our sense that a city functions as collective memory and as a crucial site of shared cultural reference depends upon its power to provide virtual as well as physical settings for interchanges among its inhabitants.

Inscribing text

None of this depends upon writing, and it all must have worked well enough in pre-literate cities. But the introduction of technologies for inscribing physical objects with text, and the associated practices of writing, distribution, and reading, created a new sort of urban information overlay. Literary theorists sometimes speak of text as if it were disembodied, but of course it isn't; it always shows up attached to particular physical objects, in particular spatial contexts, and those contexts—like the contexts of speech—furnish essential components of the meaning. A label on a wine bottle or the door to a room tells you what is inside (not what you will find in some other container), and the cover of a book refers to the pages that are physically bound to it. A stop sign at an intersection refers to that particular intersection, and you would be ill advised to argue otherwise with a traffic cop. Signing a contract has different consequences from tagging a subway wall with your name. A padlocked gate with a notice announcing, "This is not an entrance" is unremarkable, but an invitingly open door with the same sign creates a frisson of paradox and evokes memories of René Magritte.

The effects of inscription are complicated by the fact that many designed objects have characteristic, immediately recognizable forms. Unless you are instructing someone in the English language, you do not add any information by labeling a door "door," a gothic structure with a spire "church," an automobile "car," or a hot dog "hot dog." Nor is it helpful to attach pictures of doors, churches, cars, and hot dogs to these things. But labeling obviously plays a more useful role when objects have ambiguous forms, as with generic soup cans and enigmatic electronic devices. And it can combine with the message sent by the form to elaborate, clarify, add commentary, or produce irony and paradox. Designers must decide upon divisions of symbolic labor between the forms of objects and the labels and other inscriptions that they carry.

Literacy did motivate the development and proliferation of products—such as rectangular sheets of paper, scrolls, books, and billboards—that serve the primary purpose of efficiently and fairly neutrally carrying text. Indeed, if you are a clerk or a scholar, you may find that most of your attention is focused on these highly specialized textual supports. But in a modern city, almost anything that you encounter, from underwear to skyscrapers, is inscribed with a name, identification number, brand, descriptive label, warning, or instruction for use. Some urban spaces, like commercial strips, may be completely dominated by their inscriptions. Mostly, we learn what unfamiliar things are (or are supposed by someone to be) by reading the labels they carry.

It follows that the uses we put things to, and the kinds and levels of value we ascribe to them, are often highly determined by their labels—both the inscribed labels they explicitly carry and the implicit labels that result from speech and writing about them. When Alice encountered a bottle labeled "Drink me," she did just that. When a door says "Enter," we are inclined to accept the invitation. When a cigarette package warns, "Smoking kills," we think twice. Such labels, and other fragments of text that are physically associated with objects, give meaning to and are given meaning by all the other text to which they are linked by references and allusions. So the vast web of intertextual relationships that we continually navigate in our intellectual and cultural lives is inextricably interwoven with the physical objects and spatial relationships that constitute the city. Acts of use and inhabitation and acts of textual production and consumption cannot be separated neatly into functionally distinct categories, but should be understood as parts of the same system of meaning.

The system of inscriptions is shaped by the economy of surfaces. The space for text on a physical object is obviously limited; there is only so much you can inscribe on a T-shirt, a Coke can, or the label on an artifact in a museum. But this directly inscribed text can point to potentially unlimited quantities of text in other locations. The museum label might refer you to a lengthier entry in a printed catalog, and then the catalog entry might have footnotes referring to learned articles, and so on. Any labeled object can become the root of an endlessly ramifying tree of cross-linked texts. Conversely, you can follow trails of textual linkages back to particular physical objects located in particular places at particular times.

The global web of spatially grounded symbols, texts, and discourses is, as poststructuralist cultural and literary critics have emphasized, dizzyingly self-referential. You can see this, in an elementary way, in dictionary definitions of words. "Hard" and "soft" are defined as antonyms, but this does not help you much unless you can draw upon direct experience of hard or soft things to break the circularity. Natural environments must once have provided the primary basis for the grounding of language in this way. But, for thousands of years, architecture, cities, and material artifacts generally have played that role. In our urban culture, there is a reciprocal, continually evolving relationship between things that there are words for and words that there are things for. The cognitive function of architecture (distinct from its function of providing shelter) is to create a rich environment for symbol, language, and discourse grounding, and act as the glue of communication that holds communities together. One role of designers, then, is to reproduce things that there are words for—thus providing cultural continuity. But another role is to operate at the ambiguous and contested margins of the system, conceiving of things that there are not yet words for, and providing concrete referents for words that there are not yet things for.

Reproduction and telecommunication

The recording, reproduction, and telecommunication technologies of the nineteenth century added yet another set of mechanisms to the continually evolving system of symbols in space. The playwright August Strindberg was an astute early observer of this, and he vividly represented it in *Dance of Death*. The action of the play unfolds at one of the world's spatial extremities—a single room on an isolated island. This claustrophobic place initially seems to be disconnected from any wider human context. But the audience soon realizes that the walls are hung with photographs and other mementos, inserting reminders of the past into the scene. And there is a clacking telegraph apparatus in the corner, bringing news of distant happenings. By means of new technologies, information about temporally and spatially displaced events gathers at this spot, constructing a context for the two protagonists to interact and thereby allowing the playwright to disclose the complexities of their relationship.

Extending this condition on a vast scale, the mass media of the nineteenth and twentieth centuries transformed the global information dissemination system by radically separating the contexts of message transmission and reception. Novelists writing for thousands of readers, musicians in recording studios, and radio performers at their microphones could not know all of the potential reception sites for their productions, and could not assume uniformity among these sites, so they could not count on site features to help clarify or elaborate their meaning. This condition favored the production of works that were not only repeated exactly at different times or in different places, but were also as self-contained and independent of the context of reception as possible.

A closely related outcome was a growing demand for places and devices that masked the consumer's immediate surroundings in order to facilitate immersion in standardized, modular, mostly self-sufficient information structures: quiet places for undistracted reading; darkened movie theaters where all attention is focused on the screen; the white-walled, minimalist art gallery; the Walkman or iPod that plugs into your ear; and—at the logical limit—the immersive virtual reality installation. Open a book, enter a movie theater, or dial up a track on your iPod and your attention is instantly shifted to another place or time. The dense embedding of these discrete media spaces in the urban fabric yields a city that, like a film with jump cuts and flashbacks, is experienced and understood as a sequence of spatially and temporally discontinuous scenes—some of them expressions of the current, local reality, and others ephemeral media constructions.

Reproduced and displaced information also creates an overlay of anticipation and retrospection on the direct experience of places. Reading James Joyce on Dublin, Raymond Chandler on Los Angeles, or Lawrence Durrell on Alexandria before you go to these cities produces structures of expectation that may be confirmed, modified, or denied by the lived reality, while reading them after you have been there contextualizes your memories in new ways. The more you immerse yourself in texts, films, and records somehow associated with a place, the more extended and asynchronous is the process of making sense of that place and of the communication that it provides context for. I had often walked past the Pythian Temple on West 70th Street in New York, for example, and had never given it much thought until I read, in the opening paragraph of Bob Dylan's *Chronicles*, that it contained a tiny studio where Bill Haley and his Comets recorded "Rock Around the Clock." A familiar place, a record heard long ago and far away, and a newly-read text suddenly came into meaningful conjunction.

The digital era

The digital technology that emerged in the latter half of the twentieth century dramatically transformed conditions for the reproduction and transmission of information. Digital information has only a tenuous and fleeting relationship to its material substrates. It mostly exists in the form of electromagnetic charges and pulses, it moves around at incomprehensible speed, and it can be reproduced exactly and endlessly. By the dawn of the twenty-first century, it had become a ubiquitous, ghostly presence that flowed ceaselessly through global networks and lurked everywhere within the objects we encountered in our daily lives.

The containment of digital information by physical artifacts has motivated the increasingly important field of user interface design. Usually, it is most helpful to the user of a digital device to conceal behind an abstraction layer the full complexity of what is happening inside the box. The abstraction layer might be a physical cover, with the available functionality presented by an array of buttons, knobs, and the like, as with a radio or a telephone. It might be a programmed screen, with the functionality presented by means of menus and graphic symbols, as with a personal computer. Increasingly—even with very simple devices, like wall thermostats—it is both. With digital devices, form follows function—but within some framework of interface conventions, and at some chosen level of abstraction.

Digital devices rarely operate in isolation, but are linked to one another by communication channels. When some of them receive digital information emitted by others, spatially extended digital networks emerge—whether they have been planned or not. Network links may be established through physical transportation of units of portable storage such as tapes or disks (once popularly known as sneakernet), electrical or optical transmission of bits through cables, wireless transmissions through space, or by some hybrid means. Digital networks now form a vast, growing, indispensable backdrop to our everyday lives. They are connected to our thoughts and actions at interface points—locations where bits are converted to and from visible texts, images, and scenes, audible sounds, motions, vibrations, sensations of warmth and cold, and so on, much as the aural and textual worlds are connected at sites of reading aloud and transcription.

As a result, the physical settings that we inhabit are increasingly populated with spoken words, musical performances, texts, and images that have been spatially displaced from their points of origin, temporally displaced, or—as in the case of email and Web pages downloaded from servers—both spatially and temporally shifted. Physical spaces and the information space of the World Wide Web no longer occupy distinct domains—meatspace and cyberspace in the provocative trope of the cyberpunk nineties—but are increasingly closely woven together by millions of electronic devices distributed throughout buildings and cities. These devices add a dynamic layer of electronic information to the mise-en-scène established by an architectural setting and the meaningful objects and inscriptions that it contains.

The reproducibility and mobility of one particular type of digital information—computer code—also produces displacement of human agency to the networked objects that increasingly surround us. The automated teller machine that provides you with cash, the mobile phone that connects you to your mother, the automobile guidance system that gets you to your destination, and the wireless laptop computer that downloads Web pages for you are all following instructions that were formulated and issued by people you have almost certainly never met, at distant and scattered locations, at various points in the past. Furthermore, programmable objects can perform speech acts, and autonomously engage you in various forms of discourse. They can query you, demand information such as passwords, refuse you access, provide you with information, accept your instructions, and issue orders to you. They can dispense facts, fictions, and lies. And malicious computer viruses, worms, and Trojan horses can take over networked, programmable objects to do you harm.

The effects of these digitally induced dislocations, displacements, insertions, and recombinations of digital information in relation to architectural and urban settings have already been dramatic, and will become more so. A shopper once inhabited the closed world of a store, but can now make mobile phone calls to check on what's needed for dinner, or surf the Web to comparison shop. At the checkout, a wireless device can read the RFID tags on the purchased goods, charge for them, and update the inventory control and purchasing system. A political operative can stay in touch via her Blackberry and initiate action without leaving a committee room or disturbing the ongoing discussion there. A student in a seminar room once interacted primarily with the material introduced by the instructor, but can now Google the topic of discussion on a wireless laptop and focus globally accumulated information resources on the evolving discourse. A terrorist used to have to be on the scene, but now can just transmit a few bits to a mobile phone wired to some explosives.

Contrary to once-popular expectation, however, ubiquitous digital networking has not simply ironed out the differences among places, allowing anything to happen anywhere, anytime. Instead, it has provided a mechanism for the continual injection of useful information into contexts where it was once inaccessible, and where it adds a new layer of meaning.

The twenty-first century city

As these various modes and media of communication have successively taken their place in the world, they have partially substituted for their predecessors; you may, for example, choose to pick up a telephone or send an email instead of meeting a friend somewhere for a face-to-face conversation. Mostly, though, new forms of information have overlaid and complemented what had come before them. The written word did not end conversation, and the electronic word did not kill print.

All of the diverse communicative practices that I have described here—from conversation among those gathered within earshot about things at hand to inscribing and reading labels, constructing and downloading globally accessible Web pages, sending and receiving email, and blogging meetings from wireless laptops—now work together both to give meaning to places and buildings and to derive meaning from them. The social and cultural functions of built spaces have become inseparable from the simultaneous operation of multiple communication systems within and among them. Architecture no longer can (if it ever could) be understood as an autonomous medium of mass, space, and light, but now serves as the constructed ground for encountering and extracting meaning from cross-connected flows of aural, textual, and graphic, and digital information through global networks.

The following essays flesh out this view of twenty-first century buildings and cities by providing sequential snapshots of their increasingly complex, multimodal systems of spaces, information flows, and practices in operation. They were mostly written over a period extending from the bombing of Baghdad to the Bay of Bengal tsunami—the six hundred or so days of the search for the non-existent weapons of mass destruction in Iraq. With the exception of "Do We Still Need Skyscrapers?" which appeared in *Scientific American* in December 1997, and several essays that were produced for collections appearing in 2005, they were written as columns for the *Royal Institute of British Architects Journal*. They have sometimes been edited into forms slightly different from those in which they originally appeared, but the content has not been revised in the light of subsequent events.

Text and the City

1 | Do We Still Need Skyscrapers?

Our distant forebears could create remarkably tall structures by exploiting the compressive strength of stone and brick, but the masonry piles they constructed in this way contained little usable interior space. At 146 meters (480 feet), the Great Pyramid of Cheops is a vivid expression of the ruler's power, but inside it is mostly solid rock; the net-to-gross floor area is terrible. On a square base of 230 meters, it encloses the King's Chamber, which is just five meters across. The 52-meter spiraling brick minaret of the Great Mosque of Samarra does not have any interior at all. And the 107-meter stone spires of Chartres Cathedral, though structurally sophisticated, enclose nothing but narrow shafts of empty space and cramped access stairs.

The Industrial Revolution eventually provided ways to open up the interiors of tall towers and put large numbers of people inside. Nineteenth-century architects found that they could achieve greatly improved ratios of open floor area to solid construction by using steel and reinforced concrete framing and thin curtain walls. They could employ mechanical elevators to provide rapid vertical circulation. And they could integrate increasingly sophisticated mechanical systems to heat, ventilate, and cool growing amounts of interior space. In the 1870s and 1880s visionary New York and Chicago architects and engineers brought these elements together to produce the modern skyscraper. Among the earliest full-fledged examples were the Equitable Building (1868–70), the Western Union Building (1872–75) and the Tribune Building (1873–75) in New York City, and Burnham & Root's great Montauk Building (1882) in Chicago.

These newfangled architectural contraptions found a ready market because they satisfied industrial capitalism's growing need to bring armies of office workers together at locations where they could conveniently interact with one another, gain access to files and other work materials, and be supervised by their bosses. Furthermore, tall buildings fitted perfectly into the emerging pattern of the commuter city, with its high-density central business district, ring of low-density bedroom suburbs, and radial transportation systems for the daily return journey. This centralization drove up property values in the urban core and created a strong economic motivation to jam as much floor area as possible into every available lot. So as the twentieth century unfolded, and cities such as New York and Chicago grew, downtown skylines sprouted higher while the suburbs spread wider.

But there were natural limits to this upward extension of skyscrapers, just as there are constraints on the sizes of living organisms. Floor and wind loads, people, water, and supplies must be transferred to and from the ground, so the higher you go, the more of the floor area must be occupied by structural supports, elevators, and service ducts. At some point, it becomes uneconomical to add additional floors; the diminishing increment of usable floor area does not justify the additional cost.

Urban planning and design considerations constrain height as well. Tall buildings have some unwelcome effects at ground level; they cast long shadows, blot out the sky, and sometimes create dangerous and unpleasant blasts of wind. And they generate pedestrian and automobile traffic that strains the capacity of surrounding streets. To control these effects, planning authorities typically impose limits on height and on the ratio of floor area to ground area. More subtly, they may apply formulas relating allowable height and bulk to street dimensions—frequently yielding the stepped-back and tapering forms that so strongly characterize the Manhattan skyline.

The consequence of these various limits is that exceptionally tall buildings—those that really push the envelope—have always been expensive, rare, and conspicuous. So organizations can effectively draw attention to themselves and express their power and prestige by finding ways to construct the loftiest skyscrapers in town, in the nation, or maybe even in the world. They frequently find this worthwhile, even when it does not make much immediate practical sense.

There has, then, been an ongoing, century-long race for height. The Chrysler Building (319 meters) and the Empire State Building (381 meters) battled it out in New York in the late 1920s, adding radio antennas and even a dirigible mooring mast to gain their last few meters.

The contest heated up again in the 1960s and 1970s, with Lower Manhattan's World Trade Center twin towers (417 meters), Chicago's John Hancock Tower (344 meters), and finally Chicago's gigantic Sears Tower (443 meters). More recently, Cesar Pelli's skybridge-linked Petronas Twin Towers (452 meters) in Kuala Lumpur have—for a while at least—taken the title of world's tallest building.

Along the way, there were some spectacular fantasy entrants as well. In 1900 Désiré Despradelle of the Massachusetts Institute of Technology proposed a 457-meter "Beacon of Progress" for the site of the Chicago World's Fair; like Malaysia's Petronas Towers of almost a century later, it was freighted with symbolism of a proud young nation's aspirations. Despradelle's enormous watercolor rendering hung for years in the MIT design studio to inspire the students. Then, in 1956, Frank Lloyd Wright (not much more than five feet in his shoes and cape) topped it with a truly megalomaniacal proposal for a 528-story, mile-high tower for the Chicago waterfront.

While this race has been running, though, the burgeoning Digital Revolution has been reducing the need to bring office workers together face-to-face in expensive downtown locations. Efficient telecommunications have diminished the importance of centrality and correspondingly increased the attractiveness of less expensive suburban sites more convenient to the labor force. Digital storage and computer networks have increasingly supported decentralized remote access to databases rather than reliance on centralized paper files. And businesses are discovering that their marketing and public-relations purposes may now be better served by slick World Wide Web pages on the Internet and Superbowl advertising spots than by investments in monumental architecture on expensive urban sites.

We now find, more and more, that powerful corporations occupy relatively unobtrusive, low- or medium-rise suburban office campuses rather than flashy downtown towers. In Detroit, Ford and Chrysler spread themselves amid the greenery in this way—though General Motors has bucked the trend by moving into the lakeside Renaissance Center. Nike's campus in Beaverton, Oregon, is pretty hard to find, but www.nike.com is not. Microsoft and Netscape battle it out from Redmond, Washington, and Mountain View, California, respectively, and—though their logos, the look and feel of their interfaces, and their Web pages are familiar worldwide—few of their millions of customers know or care what the headquarters buildings look like. And—a particularly telling straw in the wind—Sears has moved its Chicago workforce from the great Loop tower that bears its name to a campus in far-suburban Hoffman Estates.

Does this mean that skyscrapers are now dinosaurs? Have they finally had their day? Not quite, as a visit to the fancy bar high atop Hong Kong's prestigious Peninsula Hotel will confirm. Here the washroom urinals are set against the clear plate-glass windows so that powerful men can gaze down on the city while they relieve themselves. Obviously this gesture would not have such satisfying effect on the ground floor. In the twenty-first century, as in the time of Cheops, there will undoubtedly be taller and taller buildings, built at great effort and often without real economic justification, because the rich and powerful will still sometimes find satisfaction in traditional ways of demonstrating that they're on top of the heap.

It was reality television. When all the other contestants had been voted off the island, Daniel Libeskind was left standing there, alone with his model in the lights.

Survivor, The Bachelor, Joe Millionaire, and *Fear Factor* have honed the formula. It is, by now, as rigorous as that of the sonnet. You need a cast of mostly likeable but flawed protagonists, plus a couple of obvious jerks and a few B-grade celebs. Then set them some difficult and demeaning tasks that bring them into conflict, and provide a dramatic mechanism for humiliating elimination. Even now, some ambitious cultural studies Ph.D. is probably tracing its roots to World Wrestling Federation smackdowns and writing it all up. Look for it in the Routledge spring list.

Fusion with the older form of the architectural competition was a cultural crossover waiting to happen. It began with some hardball electoral politics—an effort by the Republican Mayor Rudolph Giuliani and Republican Governor George Pataki to make sure that a hated rival, Democrat Mark Green, would not be elected mayor of New York and take control of the World Trade Center rebuilding process. Four days before the 2001 mayoral election, Pataki announced that the rebuilding effort would be directed by a new agency, the Lower Manhattan Development Corporation, with a board strongly dominated by the governor's appointees. Subsequently, during his own re-election campaign, he told a forum of victim family members what they wanted to hear: "We will never build where the towers stood." With Green safely seen off, Republican Michael Bloomberg in place as the new mayor, and Pataki back in office, the LMDC got to work.

Their first move proved to be a miscalculation. They commissioned the experienced New York firm of Beyer Blinder Belle to produce a set of massing options. These were unveiled at Federal Hall on Wall Street, and discussed at a huge public meeting in the Javits Convention Center. The public yawned—probably, in large part, because the study was presented in cool, technical format instead of as a set of realistically rendered, visionary images. People thought the abstract white models were uninspiring. Even before the proposals went public, the LMDC's chairman sensed a slagging, and preemptively announced that if they did not create "the kind of beautiful center that we want this to be, then we will change our plans."

Responding to this debacle, the LMDC went showbiz. It commissioned seven star-studded design teams (out of the 406 that had responded to a call for qualifications) to produce new schemes, and encouraged these teams to provide vivid images and models. Teams got eleven weeks to put their proposals together, and an initial stipend of $40,000—not enough to cover the cost of a good presentation model. Essentially, they were required to return the site to a close approximation of its pre-9/11 condition. The program was dominated by 6.5 to 10 million square feet of office space, to replace the 11 million that had been lost. And there was to be "a tall symbol or structure that would be recognized around the world." The results were exhibited in the Winter Garden (an atrium adjacent to the site) in December 2002 and January 2003, and evaluated by technical and financial consultants. The public presentations on December 18 highlighted a dazzling array of suit fashions, hairstyles, footwear, and eyewear for the middle-aged male, and were carried live on NY1 cable.

The architects did what good architects mostly do; they tried to solve the problem that was presented to them, and within that framework they looked for opportunities to create something of genuine, enduring cultural value. Much of it came down to convincingly packaging a vast quantity of office space, and doing so at a moment when the market for Lower Manhattan office space was crashing. The Foster team produced suave, technically and spatially sophisticated, interconnected twin towers. The home team of Richard Meier & Partners, Eisenman Architects, Gwathmey Siegel & Associates, and Steven Holl Architects proposed a gargantuan, L-shaped grid in the sky—a bit like a scaled-up fragment of the precast wall system used in Holl's recent Simmons Hall at MIT. Peterson/Littenberg did symmetrical skyscraper traditional. The young international United Architects team ringed the site with five towers that twist and meld as they rise. There's plenty of Batman's Gotham and King Kong sublime (both versions) in all of them.

After much public debate and behind-the-scenes politics, the LMDC reduced the field to two finalists, Think (a team led by Rafael Vinoly, Frederic Schwartz, Shigeru Ban, and Ken Smith), and Studio Daniel Libeskind. Think had relegated the office space to nine rather straightforward buildings surrounding the site, and had made the centerpiece of their scheme a World Cultural Center—a 1,600-foot, neo-Metabolist, latticework structure embedding cultural facilities and a memorial. Libeskind had arranged shards of office space to form the world's biggest sundial, organized to create unimpeded shafts of sunlight into transparent, commemorative spaces at the moments of the two impacts—8:46 a.m. and 10:28 a.m. every September 11. And he had been careful to control the nuances of terminology; "blocks" sound stolid, but "shards" are edgy.

Things got predictably nasty as the two teams headed for the final showdown, in full NY media glare. They hired spin-doctors. They went on the talk shows. They schmoozed with prominent members of the Families of September 11. There were Internet and magazine popularity polls. The famously venomous East Coast architectural critics zinged one-liners. There was talk of "skeletons in the sky" and "wailing walls." Scurrilous rumors circulated. Email campaigns unfolded. As decision day approached, Think seemed to be gaining ground with the professionals and the critics, but Libeskind was having better luck with the general public and the politicians.

But in the end, as the *New York Post* commented, Governor Pataki was "driving the Downtown wagon, all by himself." In late February, he announced his choice of the Libeskind scheme, which he carefully described as an "emotional protection of Ground Zero" which "brings back life to lower Manhattan." The *Post* promptly responded that it was a graveyard, a ghoulish homage, a mausoleum with a minaret in the middle, and "a blueprint so bizarre that it can't help but get better."

The main vertical element of the Libeskind scheme is a slim, spiky tower springing from the side of an office building. Its form is seductive but problematic. It needs a lot of vertical circulation, and it doesn't provide the most practical of office floor plates. (Check out the net-to-gross.) Initially, it held a garden in the sky, which was a pretty gesture, but when the developers got to work modifying the scheme this was gone in a nanosecond—replaced, sensibly enough, by telecommunications equipment, but leaving a nasty whiff of bait-and-switch.

Then there's the dopey numerology of making it 1776 feet high. Will Lord Foster respond with a 1066-meter tower in London, and restore Britain's status as Top Nation? Does Babylon's B.C. foundation date conveniently suggest going down into the ground with a bunker instead of up with a skyscraper? Maybe the developers could make the "tall symbol" a little more practical, and simultaneously extend a gesture of reconciliation to the Muslim world, by switching from the Gregorian calendar to the Hijri—which, if my calculations are correct, would get the height down to 1189 feet.

But one thing about the Libeskind scheme does seem clearly, wonderfully right. It retains and exposes the great slurry wall that had formed the foundation for the original twin towers and held back the waters of the Hudson River. This heroic piece of engineering survived the attacks, and it is an authentic, emotionally charged relic. Libeskind uses it to provide a way to go deeply into the ground, and to create a space of contemplation in the midst of commercial bustle. It is a brilliant move, and one that may hold as the development process unfolds.

Where does all this get us? There will be negotiations and compromises, and the ideas on the table will evolve out of all recognition. The men in Albany and Gracie Mansion will continue to pursue their ambitions. The Port Authority, which owns Ground Zero, is unlikely to drop its demand to jam as much commercial real estate as possible onto the site. Larry Silverstein, the holder of the leases, will not stop insisting that he has the right to rebuild as he sees fit. If I were a cynic, I might say that some talented and committed architects had been used to provide a cover of spectacle to a process that's mostly about advancing the political agendas of George Pataki and Michael Bloomberg, continuing the bottom-line planning of the Port Authority, and preserving the development opportunities of Larry Silverstein.

3 | Poison Ivy

At Washington University in St. Louis, they recently constructed a huge parking structure in the style known on American campuses as "Collegiate Gothic." It's not easy, of course, to combine a stubbornly horizontal building type with famously vertical motifs. The trick is to avoid the really pointy stuff (which costs too much anyway), and to clad the exterior with rows of flat, vaguely Tudor arches. This produces a stack of cloistered quadrangles stuffed with rusting cars. Comparing it with an unloved law school from the in-your-face concrete era, local wags like to point out that Washington University once built law schools like parking structures, but now does parking structures like law schools.

For much the same reason, the President and Fellows of Harvard annually instruct the grounds staff, in the spring, to plant Harvard Yard with new grass beneath the elms. When sentimental old alumni return for class reunions, with checkbooks at the ready, it is as sweetly green as they picture it in their memories. American colleges and universities are in the nostalgia theme park business. Trustees call it tradition. The student recruitment and fundraising people know that it's about enlisting architecture to brand a product. If you're selling entry to the ivied establishment (or reassurance of continued membership), you want the customers to know it.

At Princeton, they are as careful about theming as the Disney Corporation. The incomparable Ralph Adams Cram got them into the game, around 1900, by introducing elegantly detailed Tudor Gothic quadrangles. The students loved them, and Woodrow Wilson, Princeton's president at the time, approvingly commented that they "added a thousand years to the history of Princeton." As the twentieth century unfolded, the suburban New Jersey campus frequently wobbled into modernism—some of it distinguished—but the trustees have now mandated a return to the Cramesque for the twenty-first. Volkswagen is building Beetles again, and BMW is building Minis (with a successful move upmarket in both cases), so why can't Princeton build Gothic?

Of course, you cannot just replicate Cram these days. As with retro cars, there are new standards and requirements to accommodate. For one thing, you have to provide elevator access for those with disabilities, so you end up stringing the student rooms along double-loaded corridors instead of clustering them around stairways—a spatial organization that is more Motel 6 than medieval. Compared to a thousand, or even a hundred years ago, there will be a lot more plumbing and shower stalls to jam in somewhere. Fireplaces are out of the question (too dangerous), and as for operable windows, they pose a suicide risk—not to mention an opportunity to toss out the furniture, like Russell Crowe in *A Beautiful Mind*: better just go for standard HVAC. Desks? Don't imagine that the freshmen, sophomores, and seniors will be silently poring over texts like the Venerable Bede: they will be surfing the Web on their wireless laptops, listening through headphones to MPG files downloaded from KaZaA, and pinging SMS flirtation to one another—simultaneously.

The truth is that the branding is all in the wrapper. Inside, a different logic takes over. As parents who trundle their kids off on the college application tour quickly discover, today's dorm rooms hardly vary from sea to shining sea. It's not surprising: they mostly respond to the same surveys and focus-groups, use the same technologies, and get held to the same cost-per-bed numbers plugged into the same spreadsheet business models. The product is as generic as bottled water, so—as the marketing gurus will tell you—you get into a game of distinctive labeling, associating yourself with the images and lifestyles that appeal to your target demographics, and differentiating yourself from your competitors.

But there are, in the end, some crucial differences between Classic Coke and Gothic Princeton. Historic fancy dress can be fun for a while, and can provide welcome opportunities for irony, contradiction, and witty transgression. But if you strut around garbed like Henry VII all the time, you quickly become a tiresome bore. Similarly, fancy-dress architecture flirts with the sin of pretentious affectation. Do the world's most privileged undergraduates really need that?

Then, there's the treacherous messiness of metonymy. Evoke the virtues of some particular point in the past, and others may recall its vices. (Just ask Senator Trent Lott.) Exactly what *were* the social attitudes of Ivy League gentlemen circa 1900? Weren't their faces uniformly white (in contrast to the kitchen help)? Where were the women? What if you were gay? What about the endemic anti-Semitism? Creditably, great institutions like Princeton have moved on. So isn't it just a bit unseemly, today, to identify with that moment? It's like flying the Confederate flag over Southern statehouses.

Most importantly, institutions of higher learning have a responsibility to be more than lifestyle marketing organizations. Their business, they would claim, is the rigorous, critical, adventurous investigation of ideas—so why not in architecture, just as in scholarship and science? If they believe their own rhetoric, they should take major campus construction projects as exciting opportunities to probe and rethink the nature of their communities, to reflect upon their relationships to larger society, to respond in some articulate way to a cultural moment, and to add layers to the complex, multigenerational discourses that campuses represent. They would not give tenure to a professor who merely recycled the same old stuff between covers calibrated for maximum marketability, and they should not give campus space to buildings that do no better.

Steven Holl's new Simmons Hall, on the MIT campus in Cambridge, Massachusetts, brilliantly demonstrates that the more intellectually ambitious path remains possible—as it was when Thomas Jefferson planned the University of Virginia, when Alvar Aalto designed MIT's Baker House, and when Charles Moore and his colleagues did Kresge College for the University of California at Santa Cruz in the 1960s. It is not a perfect building: the cost escalated to a troublesome extent, the structure is not particularly rational, and there are some details that don't really work. But it is a brave and passionate one (for which we must credit both the vision of the architect and the determined idealism of MIT's President Charles Vest), and it is bursting with ideas.

Unlike the houses of Harvard Yard, it is not in the bricks-and-ivy, four hundred years of history part of Cambridge. It is squarely on the other side of the tracks—built on a flat expanse of fill, right beside a railway line, in a decayed and obsolete industrial area that is currently being reborn as a biotech hotspot. It is not about the comfortable continuity of tradition (specially for those who have been privileged by it), but about transformation and social mobility—not about fitting in, but breaking out. It wants to attract the first-generation migrant kids whose parents have worked long hours to get them into college and on course for a better life, the children of blue-collar families who start with little but make it on sheer merit, the high school misfits who will thrive when they reach the company of others as smart as they are. Appropriately then, it avoids culture-specific motifs and class-bound imagery (except, maybe, for a hint of Corb), and employs an exterior vocabulary of rigorously abstract forms that doesn't even give you much clue, from a distance, about the true scale. It is what you choose to make of it, and it takes some work.

At first glance, the plan is just a straightforward rendition of the ubiquitous double-loaded corridor. But it turns out, on closer inspection, to be splattered with free-form blobs. And, in section, these reveal themselves as sinuous wormholes snaking up through the floors, creating a marvelous system of unexpected interconnections and informal social spaces.

The real jaw-dropper, though, is in the endlessly inventive animation through light and color. The deeply revealed, gridded façade provides shifts from apparent solidity to airy openness, from neutral to vividly hued, and from reflective to sharply shadow-lined as you move on by. Hundreds of tiny operable windows end up at varied horizontal angles to morning and evening sun, providing changing patterns of glitter and dazzle for passing joggers. The aluminum cladding responds subtly to the shifting balance of cloudy sky and the snowy ground. At night, the square openings with their individual curtains read like pixels. Inside, there are pretty moves with meshed metal screens and colored lights diffused by perforated plywood. And, in the individual rooms, you encounter the surprising warmth of curved, polished plywood furniture—homage to Aalto across the athletic fields.

And what's the lesson for all those crusty old trustees? Forget about mandating historic styles—which is as silly and stultifying as requiring email to be written in Shakespearean English! Leave the logo-led marketing to the T-shirt and coffee mug vendors! Architecture can do more for you than that.

4 | The Cobblestones and the Beach

Australia has many Greeks and Italians, but no agoras or piazzas. Oz has been figuring out its own, new-world ways to make public space.

It began with beaches. This is hardly surprising in a country that was colonized from the sea, is prodigally endowed with golden sand, and enjoys plenty of beautiful beach weather. Of the major cities, only the bush capital Canberra and the climatically challenged Hobart and Darwin miss out on these urban ready-mades. Sydney and Brisbane make much of their public life on the Pacific Ocean, Melbourne and Adelaide on the Southern, and Perth on the Indian. Go to Bondi or Portsea on a good day, or to any of scores of other great strips of shore, and you will see a dense, lively, no-worries mix of zinc-creamed kids and sundried oldies, beer guts and gym-toned muscles, surfers and snoozers, flesh-flaunting microwear and baggy shorts, Ockers and immigrants—the lot. The beaches are genuinely democratic places to meet, to talk, to see and be seen, and just to hang out with a crowd.

When the colonials got around to some serious urban design in the nineteenth century, they appropriated comfortingly familiar British models. So the booming new cities were fitted out with street grids and tree-lined main boulevards, greenbelts, and garden squares with war memorials and statues of Queen Victoria. This layer of old-world stuff was generously done, and mostly pretty good—particularly so today, when the oaks and elms, Moreton Bay figs, and Norfolk Island pines have splendidly matured. It provided room for cricket grounds, football fields, tennis stadiums, and jogging tracks—gracefully accommodating the Australian obsession with sport. And, in Colonel William Light's layout of Adelaide, it yielded one undeniable masterpiece of urban spatial composition.

The nineteenth and early twentieth centuries were also eras of pragmatic infrastructure construction. Docks and warehouses, railway yards, and tram yards were unsentimentally plonked down wherever it seemed most convenient. More recently, as the need for such facilities in inner urban areas has diminished and as the demand for urban amenity has grown in the increasingly sybaritic Lucky Country (you need *some* place to drink all that shiraz and chardy), the reclamation of these sites has provided opportunities to add a third layer of public space.

In this third wave, Sydney tore down the old tram sheds on Bennelong Point and built Utzon's Opera House, spruced up the shabby old ferry terminal at Circular Quay, and created a sunny, bustling shoreline space that links the downtown urban grid to the stunning harbor. Brisbane wove new connections to its wide, silvery river. And, over the last decade or so, Melbourne has radically transformed itself by excising drab encrustations of

nineteenth-century infrastructure and obsolete industrial buildings, constructing new commercial and cultural facilities and
public spaces in their place, and using these as pedestrian con-
nectors to its historic docklands and the Yarra River. The latest
piece of this puzzle to click into place is Federation Square—the
outcome of an international competition won by a young team
under the name of Lab Architecture Studio.

Federation Square sits right at the crossroads of
Melbourne—the busy intersection of Swanston and Flinders
Streets, and the place where leafy St. Kilda Road heads off across
Prince's Bridge for the bayside beaches. The great, domed, polychromed stucco pile of the Flinders Street main railway station
occupies one of the four corners. If you turn clockwise, the next
corner is the site of Young and Jackson's famous old pub, and
the longtime home of Chloe—a pearly-pink, soft-core, male-
gaze-grabbing, French academic nude (Jules Lefebvre, 1875) who
hangs in the bar. Third is William Butterfield's learnedly detailed
gothic revival St. Paul's Cathedral, done in polychrome masonry.
Finally, there is a space that was incongruously occupied by the
vast expanse of the Jolimont railway yards, garnished at the
edge, until nobody could bear looking at them any more, by
some truly dreadful sixties office towers. These yards have now
been decked over to continue Melbourne's urban fabric to the
banks of the Yarra and to form the new square.

The anchor attractions are a major gallery of Australian
art, the Australian Center for the Moving Image, and outdoor
performance spaces. The plan extends the rhythms of surveyor
Robert Hoddle's original Melbourne grid, but gives them some
hip-hop twists, and unzips itself at the navel to reveal a stone-

paved plaza. The building surfaces—polychromed like their historic neighbors—are clad in sandstone, zinc, and glass on metal frames, pulled back every now and again, like fashionably ripped jeans, to reveal another layer beyond. But the facade panels, instead of following some familiar architectural logic, are triangles organized within a pinwheel grid that looks non-repeating, at least until you painstakingly figure it out. It's all sharp-edged patches of varied fleshtone, the effect of tanlines on bared summer skin.

The focal point isn't a monument, a stage, or a podium to address the masses. It's a giant LED video screen—showing, when I was last there, tennis live from the Australian Open.

It works: the crowds are there in the numerous open-air cafes, contentedly scoffing cappuccinos. It goes beyond straight-forward appropriation from Mother Earth and the Mother Country to confront—boldly and mostly successfully—the problem of public space for a postcolonial, multicultural, electronically networked society. Its European roots are apparent, but it has gone spare, edgy, and brown under southern skies—approximately the look that Chloe would get if she dropped a few kilos, got some tats and a little sun, bleached her hair, and learned a few hip-hop moves.

And it isn't just about coffee and spectacle—which could, after all, be provided by shopping malls and Disneyworlds. The creation of true public space is a city's affirmation of essential freedoms—of assembly, expression, and dissent. The people of Melbourne get it. On February 14, more than 150,000 of them marched through the streets to gather, in opposition to war in Iraq, in Federation Square.

The Baghdad of the Abbasid caliphs, founded in 762, was a perfectly circular walled city. The maimed and dying now jamming Baghdad's hospitals would not be comforted by the irony, but it was originally called Madinat al-Salam—"City of Peace."

Ancient and medieval walled cities—of which Baghdad briefly rose to the top of the global heap in the era of Harun al-Rashid—co-evolved with contemporary weapons technology. A high, strong barrier served well enough against bad guys with swords. Add a moat or similar device to keep besiegers at a distance, and that took care of primitive projectiles as well. Concentrated, sedentarized populations within could protect their lives and their accumulating assets from nomadic bandits and mobile armies without. The sheer power of massed numbers provided economic and cultural advantage, enabled the division of labor, and created an incentive to further growth.

Eventually, as Louis Mumford so elegantly recounted in *The Culture of Cities*, the rise of capitalism created a new constellation of economic forces that "favored expansion and dispersal in every direction, from overseas colonization to the building up of new industries, whose technological improvements simply canceled out all medieval restrictions." For emerging modern cities, "the demolition of their urban walls was both practical and symbolic."

And, of course, the military technology of the industrial era made urban walls irrelevant anyway. The transportation infrastructure and mechanized vehicles that powered trade and economic growth could also mobilize military forces on a fearsome scale. Chemical engineering cranked up the production of explosives to whatever levels the generals might find necessary. The output of steelworks and heavy engineering plants provided both skyscrapers and tanks. Assembly-line production of warplanes opened the possibility of massive attack from the air. By the 1920s, strategic destruction of urban and regional systems—particularly by carefully targeted bombing—was the obvious alternative to the old-fashioned siege or the gruesome stalemate of trench warfare. The idea was to get out the land use and transportation maps that the planners had so obligingly prepared (or the aerial photographs when these were not available), figure out where your enemies were most vulnerable, and destroy their means of production and distribution and their morale.

It all came together at Guernica, in April 1937. Nazi bombers delivered 100,000 pounds of shock and awe to the small Basque village, and simultaneously signaled to the world that you were either for them or against them. Most of the town was destroyed, and 1,600 people were killed or wounded. It was, as it turned out, a practice run for bigger things.

By May 1, in the midst of huge anti-fascist protests in Paris, Picasso had begun work on his great painting inspired by black-and-white news photographs of the atrocity. Three months later he delivered it to the Spanish Pavilion at the Paris Exposition. The Pavilion, by Jose Luis Sert, was a modest structure overshadowed by Albert Speer's looming German Pavilion, and was not even shown on the official maps. The Exposition was intended to celebrate the triumphs of modern technology, so the Spanish Republic's attempt to focus attention on the horrors of modern warfare was not well received by the other exhibitors. The German fair guide dismissed *Guernica* as "a hodgepodge of body parts that any four-year-old could have painted." But within a few years, the world had been forced to confront the industrialized slaughter in the Third Reich death camps, the horrors of the London blitz, the reduction of Dresden to scorched rubble, and the instant vaporization of Hiroshima and Nagasaki.

Nowadays, we are not so crude. The co-evolution of urbanism, technology, and military strategy has moved to a new stage. In this era of miniaturized electronics and global digital networks, we map cities with GIS systems and satellite surveillance, and express locations of buildings in GPS coordinates; this serves us both for automobile navigation systems and missile guidance. Sophisticated electrical, telecommunication, and computer networks allow large, modern cities like Baghdad to function with extraordinary efficiency, but you can immediately paralyze these cities by taking their networks down. Security think tanks—impressed by the digital revolution in commerce and industry, social life, and culture—push for a similar revolution in military affairs. Desk warriors look for opportunities to test their new theories of cyberwar, smart weapons, the information edge, the networked battlefield, and victory through zapping and swarming rather than massed attack. And spin doctors know that it is not world's fairs that matter now, but global news networks and the World Wide Web.

As the United Nations was impatiently swept aside, and the long-sought war on Iraq begun, Pentagon spokesmen talked smoothly of electronically picking out legitimate military targets, precision strikes, and the minimization of civilian casualties. This gave grim amusement to architects who know how buildings are put together, and how careful you have to be about life safety at the best of times. (Building code compliance is not much help with a cruise missile in the lobby.) No matter how current your electronically-delivered intelligence, how smart your weapons, and how precise your aim, you cannot detonate high explosives inside buildings without killing and injuring large numbers of innocent inhabitants. The American authorities were not interested in keeping track of the toll, and the Iraqis quickly lost the capacity to do so, but the Baghdad morgues were soon heaped with scorched, mangled, and dismembered bodies.

Few will weep for the atrocious Saddam, least of all the ordinary Iraqis who suffered terribly under his rule. But he will soon seem a sideshow to a much larger story—the twenty-first century's redefinition of the relationship of cities to prevailing technology and the violent expression of power. We may well look back to see that Baghdad was the electronically networked world's Guernica, and Al Jazeera (which was not afraid to show body parts) its Picasso.

The ruined monastery of San Lazaretto, on an island in the Venice lagoon, is a grim and spooky place. For centuries, from the days of the fourteenth-century Black Death, this was Venice's quarantine outpost—the place where incoming ships suspected of carrying plague were detained for forty days (*quaranta giorni*) before discharging their cargo.

In general, you can see what really scares a society—its collective vision of the dangerous other—by examining its architectural arrangements for exclusion and isolation. The Venetians, understandably, were terrified of seafarers bringing deadly infection, so an island isolation center run by compliant monks made obvious sense. On land, city walls were the traditional exclusion devices: inside, the good citizens went about their business, while outside were Vikings, Saracens, brigands, Achilles and lots of pissed-off Greeks, or whatever. The scheme is beautifully depicted in the Lorenzetti Allegories of Good and Bad Government in the Palazzo Pubblico of Siena.

The standard story is that gunpowder, transportation systems, and capitalism did away with city walls. But of course they didn't, really. I am reminded of the old story of the topologist who wants to cage a lion that is frisking around somewhere. She simply prepares the cage enclosure, stands inside, and then inverts the universe. Now, the lion is inside the cage—along with a lot of other stuff—and the topologist is safely on the exterior. (There may be some construction problems: the walls have presumably been turned inside out, like a sweaty sock stripped off your foot.) Modern cities have performed a similar topological inversion. The good citizens are now *outside*, while the feared others are concentrated, as far as can be managed, within jail walls.

It is instructive to enumerate the categories of exclusion, and the justifications that are offered. In *A Journal of the Plague Year*, for example, Daniel Defoe described the practice of "locking up the doors of people's houses, and setting a watchman there night and day to prevent their stirring out or any coming to them." Those who got penned in with plague victims were "very clamorous and uneasy at first, and several violences were committed and injuries offered to the men who were set to watch the houses so shut up." But, Defoe concluded, "It was a public good that justified the private mischief."

The private mischief is often compounded—sometimes egregiously—by the tendentious conflation of categories. During the 1892 epidemics of typhus and cholera in New York, more than a thousand healthy immigrants (mostly Russian Jews) were quarantined on North Brother Island. Fear of disease provided convenient cover for anti-immigrant, anti-Semitic politics, and was a brutally effective way of keeping newcomers out of the job market.

After Pearl Harbor there was Manzanar, a place for removal of Japanese Americans from Los Angeles, San Francisco, and other cities in an "exclusion area" that ran down the West Coast from Canada to Mexico. On a bleakly beautiful site sloping up into the Sierras (now as ruined and silent as San Lazaretto), it was a territory outside city limits and outside normal protections of the law. Architecturally, it was a direct, huts-and-wire descendent of the Roman *castrum*—a type that has served our modern culture well for internment camps, POW camps, death camps, gulags, and Guantanamo Bay. There may be differences in conceptions of the public good that serve as justification, and in degrees of private mischief that result, but these are all variations on the theme of forced, militarized banishment from urban life.

Stone and iron jails and asylums (sorry, correctional and psychiatric facilities) are the traditional urban repositories of the dangerous other. They can even add to civic grandeur, as with Henry Hobson Richardson's Allegheny County Courthouse and Jail in Pittsburgh—a masterpiece of the punitive sublime. Their recurrent problem, though, is that they start to overflow whenever societies wax enthusiastic about incarceration. Eighteenth-century London tried to solve the problem by pressing hulks on the Thames into service as prisons. When these overflowed as well, it proved convenient to transport thieves, whores, and Irishmen to Australia. As young black males crowd America's prisons, Washington's criminal justice policy pundits no doubt eye that option with envy.

In recent decades, the feared and unwanted refugee has emerged as a leading exemplar of the dangerous other, and the refugee camp has taken its place as a characteristic building type of our time. There are informally constructed and relatively permeable versions, such as those of Lebanon, the West Bank, and Gaza. Then there are the fenced and guarded refugee detention camps in Australia and other more affluent and attractive refugee destinations. The boat people, immigration queue jumpers, and potential terrorists (including the children) who have recently fetched up on Australia's shores have been tossed into remote, razor-wired detention centers at Woomera, Baxter, and Port Hedland.

None of this works, though, for the latest object of urban fear—the SARS carrier. True, some public health officials have attempted plague-house-like lockdowns of hospitals where SARS has been detected. And known SARS cities, like Hong Kong and Singapore, have been slapped with travel warnings and bans. But travelers move much faster, now, than in the days of San Lazaretto. The global air transportation network allows SARS carriers to fly to the far side of the globe and merge with the populations of new cities before they show any obvious signs of illness. Furthermore, expectations have changed, and the global economy depends upon free and rapid transfer of people and goods, so forty-day detentions on arrival are no longer a realistic option on a large scale—even if we could quickly build the necessary quarantine facilities.

Anthrax and letter bombs in the mail, sarin in the subway, underground terrorists who hijack airliners, nuclear devices in shipping containers, and viruses in computer networks present similar problems. The characteristic threats of the globally networked world move quickly, often in undetectable and unstoppable ways, once they infiltrate the networks. They create a state of global, distributed siege from which no city escapes. This requires network access nodes—from airport departure gates to air intakes, fire hydrants, and machines in computer networks— to enact new forms of high-tech detection and defense strategies. These network nodes are the new sites for identification and exclusion of the dangerous other—freighted with all the moral complexities and opportunities for mischief that this entails.

I just saw Palladio in the piazza of Vicenza. I listened as he most eloquently described the process of designing and constructing the Basilica Palladiana—the "palace game," as he called it—and afterwards we had dinner. It was, of course, a play—one that provoked reflection on portrayals of architects on stage and screen, and how these disclose cultural shifts and fault-lines.

Occasionally Hollywood has offered us an architect as romantic lead. Who can forget Gary Cooper—first shown brooding, sweaty, and shirtless in a quarry—as Howard Roark in *The Fountainhead*? The sex isn't explicit (this was 1949, after all) but there's that episode with the throbbing rock drill, and Patricia Neal does mount Roark's (even Freud might blush) tower in the climactic scene. In the awful 1983 remake of *Breathless*, the heroine is allegedly a UCLA architecture student, though there is scant evidence of that: the very beautiful Valérie Kaprisky has the principal plot function of casting smoldering glances at the very beautiful Richard Gere and removing her clothing as frequently as possible. In *The Towering Inferno*, Paul Newman casts smoldering glances at a smoldering building while O. J. Simpson rescues a kitten.

On television, architect shows haven't stacked up well against doctor, lawyer, and cop shows. Maybe it's because the employees of today's corporate architecture firms haven't established such a plausible professional lock on the big existential questions of life and death, truth and justice, or whatever. You could, perhaps, imagine an architectural version of *The West Wing*—with super-articulate, fast-talking, fast-walking, Prada-clad job captains passionately debating issues of plot ratio, service core layout, and value engineering. And I could see *American Academy in Rome* as a reality show, with fellows getting voted out of the villa.

In the 1970s the most famous architect on American television was Mike Brady of *The Brady Bunch*. Mike had a perky blonde wife, three blonde daughters from her previous marriage, three brunette sons from his, and a firm with projects in distant locations—providing a convenient excuse to take the show on location. The scripts were big on pat ethical dilemmas, like cases in a professional practice seminar. Mike once landed a courthouse job on a site in a local park—only to discover that the wife and kids were leading the local greenies in a campaign against the project. What was he to do?

Wilbur Post, the leading two-legged character of the sixties sitcom *Mister Ed*, was always getting upstaged by the talking horse. If I understand the relationship correctly—and Wilbur's wife Carol did find it puzzling—Wilbur was the design partner and Ed the marketing partner in an architectural firm operating out of Ed's stable. Ed suffered the usual indignities of marketing. In Episode 113, according to the definitive source *Mister Ed Online*, "A shopping mall investor needs an architect, and Wilbur is suggested. When the 300-pound investor wants to ride Ed, Wilbur sees no problem."

Martin Gray, the recently Pritzkered, fifty-something protagonist of Edward Albee's 2002 Tony-winning *The Goat, or Who is Sylvia?* clearly has a more upscale professional life than Wilbur. It is the booming nineties, and he has just been selected to design "The World City, the two hundred billion dollar dream city of the future." He also has a bigger relationship problem, though. In the pivotal scene he confesses to his wife that he has fallen in love with Sylvia—a goat. A fair amount of vase tossing and apartment trashing ensues. But nobody sleeps with a horse, of course, unless of course, the horse . . . well, probably not in Wilbur and Ed's Eisenhower-era suburbia.

It is a tempting mise-en-scène to put a famous architect into one of his own buildings and have him tell the audience all about it. You can even use the architect's own words, but you have to be sure there's enough material. Minimalist modernism doesn't help. Even Samuel Becket couldn't make much of "Less is more" (exit puffing cigar).

Palladio did leave plenty of material. And in *Il Giuoco del Palazzo* or *Palladio in Piazza*, which has been playing in Vicenza's Basilica this spring, that very building's story unfolds within the cavernous interior itself. The script (published by Marsilio Editori, Venice) is by Howard Burns, the distinguished historian of renaissance architecture from the University of Venice. Gianfranco de Bosio—who will be remembered by Italian film buffs for the classic *Il Terrorista*—directs a lively and intelligent cast.

As the author's preface notes, it is an exercise in historical neo-realism—an effort to recover the past by engaging not only its documents and narratives, but also its actual language, its ideas and patterns of thought, and its material culture. The acknowledged inspirations are Walter Scott's novel *Old Mortality* and Roberto Rossellini's film masterpiece *The Rise to Power of Louis XIV*. Much of the text is constructed, with extraordinary ingenuity and erudition, from cinquecento documents, and the characters mostly speak in Vicentine dialect.

Brilliantly colored period costumes (except for architects and Calvinists in sober black), the unmistakably Italian features of the actors, and high-contrast lighting pop the scenes into a convincingly Titianesque visual register. The set is a one-to-one replica of an arched bay from Palladio's loggia. Architectural drawings relating to the current action are projected, life-size, onto cyclorama screens, and much of the action focuses on a huge wooden model of the Basilica that various architects and their supporters use to display alternative schemes. The atmosphere is rigorously cinquecento classical, but there is also a sly postmodern game of representation within representation within representation: when you step out into the actual loggia at intermission—to see kids on skateboards in the piazza and cyclists imperturbably blabbing into cellphones—it just doesn't seem real anymore.

This is a play of interwoven ideas about the craft of stone masonry, the exigencies of construction, the making of cities, the contradictions of public life, the presence of the past, and the flow of hope and mortality. You get to see Giulio Romano as an overpaid, condescending structural consultant, Palladio as a fervent salesman for his project, Vincenzo Scamozzi as a bitterly envious pedant, and lots of Thienes and Valmaranas with swords. There is a nodding old councillor who responds to flights of architectural theory with "I'm going to take a pee." The last words go to the intrepid *inglese* Inigo Jones, in a speech modeled on Ben Jonson's response to the death of Shakespeare: "Bramante e Michelangelo sono i suoi compari; Vitruvio un fratello." He was not just for one epoch, but for all times. His "noblissima Vicenza," a city that honors its citizens, has inspired the world.

Wilbur Post probably goes down better in Crawford, Texas. He has moral clarity. He says what he means and means what he says. When in doubt, he listens to the voice of Ed. But *Il Giuoco del Palazzo* represents the sort of complex, resonant, certainty-challenging cultural moment that decadent old Europe still manages incomparably well. Bravo!

As the cover story for the invasion of Iraq began to unravel, I tried a modest experiment. Each morning, with the last of my coffee, I would type, "Bush lies" into Google. On June 24 this netted me 731,000 hits. A couple of days later the number was up to 768,000. Despite Steve Bell's repeated pants-on-fire cartoons in the *Guardian*, Tony Blair's total has not spiked quite so spectacularly; "Blair lies" first yielded 249,000, and then the harvest jumped to 258,001—drawing away from "Saddam lies" at 240,000. (Some of this might have resulted from commentary on the hundredth anniversary of George Orwell's birth, but the effect was probably insignificant; you rarely find "lies" mentioned in the same sentence as *that* Blair.) When I last checked the score, on the Fourth of July, Bush had just broken 800,000—racking them up faster than an opener in a one-day international, and clearly headed for his million—while his British sidekick was plugging along at 279,000. For calibration purposes I tried "Gandhi lies," and did get a handful of hits, but these mostly turned out to refer to Indira, Rajiv, and Sonia, and the first for Mohandas was his famous aphorism:

"Satisfaction lies in the effort, not in the attainment, full effort is full victory."

This is a simple example of a technique that's known in the software trade as data mining. You take some massive database, apply software to trawl through it, and draw inferences—with, of course, varying levels of confidence—from the results. In particular, you watch out for patterns and trends.

Credit card companies have long used such software to look for suspicious patterns of customer behavior. If your card simultaneously logs bar bills in New York and Bangkok, for example, chances are there's something wrong, and you're likely to get a phone call to check. Similarly, Amazon.com analyzes your buying patterns, and uses the results to make book and CD recommendations next time you surf in. And, since the September 11 attacks, American three-letter agencies have shown a lot of interest in cross-connecting databases, increasing electronic surveillance, and employing large-scale data mining to identify the enemy; no doubt they were stung by the famous *Onion* headline, "U.S. Vows To Defeat Whoever It Is We're At War With." Admiral John Poindexter, who was convicted for his Watergate lies back in the Nixon era, has been leading the charge.

Now the world of data mining is intersecting that of architecture. The crucial enabling technology is that of the RFID tag—a pinhead-sized wireless transponder that costs pennies and can be embedded in just about anything, from consumer products to pets. When you ping a RFID tag with a suitable RF (radio frequency) signal, it returns a unique ID number. Thus it is much like the familiar barcode, except that it can be read silently, invisibly, and at a distance. In conjunction with suitable readers, RFID tags connect everyday physical things to the Internet, allowing information about them to be both collected and delivered. They start to become, in terminology popularized by the MIT Media Laboratory, things that think. Soon they will be everywhere; Gillette recently caused a stir by ordering half a billion of them to embed in razorblade packages and other such products.

A closely related technology, which provides the capacity to think a little more, is that of the miniaturized wireless sensor. You can set up such sensors to detect heat, light, motion, pressure, radiation, biotoxins, the presence of a car in a parking space, or pretty much anything else that might be of interest. Furthermore, you can provide them with onboard processing power, wireless communication capability, and the capacity to self-organize themselves into wireless sensor nets. They are becoming so tiny and cheap that you will be able to scatter them around like rice at a wedding. Joe Paradiso of the Media Lab has proposed packing them so tightly into sheet materials that they form sensate skins with capabilities much like those of our own skins.

RFID tags, sensors, distributed intelligence, and wireless networking technologies are combining to create the possibility of buildings that continually draw inferences about their inhabitants and respond accordingly. In Cambridge, Massachusetts, not far from the Media Lab, architect Kent Larson is currently constructing PlaceLab—an apartment that thinks—to critically explore the implications of this. PlaceLab is loaded with tags and sensors, and harvests an enormous flood of information, which is then mined for inferences about the current condition and needs of its inhabitants.

PlaceLab has an eminently worthy social goal—to find new ways of providing inexpensive, effective, in-home health care for the aging baby-boomers. If it works out as expected, it will sensitively adjust lighting and interior climate in response to your current activities, send out an alarm if it detects that you have fallen down, discreetly remind you to take your medication, and reflect on your eating and exercise habits and—like an attentive personal trainer—intervene on occasion with helpful tips. I will happily sign up for all that. But I will not want the data stream to go to my medical insurance provider, and I'll be damned if I'll let it go to Admiral Poindexter's database apparatchiks. The point of PlaceLab is not only to explore the emerging technology of places that think, but also to investigate the ethical and policy issues that this technology raises, and the design expression and practical implementation of appropriate privacy and other principles. It is the most crucial new issue to emerge in architecture for a very long time.

Meanwhile, if you want to join the critical discourse around this topic, check out the Media Lab's Government Information Awareness site at opengov.media.mit.edu—which was, appropriately, born on the Fourth of July. It announces: "Modeled on recent government programs designed to consolidate information on individuals into massive databases, our system does the opposite, allowing you to scrutinize those in government. Citizens are able to explore data, track events, find patterns, and build risk profiles, and motivate action. We like to think of it as a Citizen's Intelligence Agency." Pennsylvania Avenue and Downing Street may not care for this sort of scrutiny, but hey, if they've done nothing wrong, they've got nothing to worry about.

Summer on Cape Cod is a tableau vivant reminder of the PC-free remark—by Gore Vidal, Mark Twain, Donald Rumsfeld, or some such legendary humorist—that America is a nation of fat people ruled by thin people. (Teddy Kennedy in Hyannis splendidly aside, of course.) The svelte and privileged have trust-fund tans, live in big houses by the water, and drive fancy SUVs or cute little ragtops. The sunburned lumpen-whatever, as I recently discovered, take their Chevys and pickups to the Wellfleet drive-in.

As I sat with a Jeep full of pajama-clad kids, watching *Finding Nemo* and munching through a mega-tub of butter-smeared popcorn, I reflected that the drive-in is high on the endangered architectural species list. Its habitat of cheap, suburban fringe land and leatherette-bench-seat, pride-of-Detroit gas-guzzlers is rapidly disappearing. The housewife-and-bread-winner nuclear family, for which these sheetmetal saurians were intended, isn't doing so well either. But the big outdoor screen has mostly been done in by electronics and advanced telecommunication—first television, then digital delivery systems. Why drive miles to breathe exhaust fumes and squint through a bug-spattered windshield when you can get the Disney Channel on cable, or just rent a DVD? This one may hang on for a little longer by shamelessly hamming it up with retro graphics, and pitching itself to nostalgic baby-boomers, but its days are clearly numbered.

The Cape turns out, in fact, to be a museum of building types that emerged and thrived in the early automobile era, but are now nearing extinction. Life is sleepier here, so those famous Schumpeterian cycles of creative destruction crank slower. There is still, for instance, a terrific collection of faded motels, spreading long, low wings out on either side of taller central pavilions, like the barchesse of Palladian villas. My favorite is on Route 6 at Orleans, where you can see exactly how new functional wine has ended up in old formal bottles—classical detailing (well, sort of), strict bilateral symmetry, motel office and restaurant in the piano nobile, bedrooms in place of the barnyard animals. Others are done in the white clapboard box order, or fishnet-and-driftwood with plastic lobster. But the jig is up. As the seemingly endless construction of holiday homes and retirement dream houses continues, and as the value of scarce seaside land is inexorably driven higher (even while the wider economy stumbles), these relics return too few dollars per square foot to survive.

Sadly, we will soon kiss goodbye to these campy old things, with their gaudy makeup; they will simply be bulldozed to make way for shopping malls and condo complexes. But sturdier, more respectable stuff gets saved and born again. In the early industrial era, many Massachusetts towns grew up around solid brick mills, but these were eventually abandoned as burgeoning transportation networks and energy distribution systems allowed industrial production to disperse, and as cheaper labor could be found elsewhere. Then, in the tech boom years of the more recent past, they were rehabilitated and modernized to accommodate electronics, software, and biotechnology companies. At Salem, home of the notorious witch-hunts, the vast former shoe factory that dominates the waterfront was remade for the new economy. At North Adams in the Berkshires, an old textile factory complex has become the Mass MoCA contemporary art museum, together with industrial tenant space offering, the Web site boasts, "the warmth and solid feel of 19th-century mill buildings . . . combined with plug-and-play telecommunications connectivity and clean, reliable electrical supply." It's a bit like New Labor. Now that the go-go nineties have gone, forlorn for-lease signs are up on many of these structures once more.

The local bank buildings that used to anchor Main Streets have gone the way of floppy disk drives. These were often solid and handsome structures, by architects of distinction, designed not only to store the money and accommodate the bank's activities, but also to represent its power and prestige in the community. But as the retail action shifted from downtown to big-box stores with parking lots on the edge of town, walk-up banks were challenged by rivals with drive-up tellers on commercial strips by the highway. Then cash machines began to appear everywhere—in supermarkets, gas stations, airports, casinos, and just about anywhere else you might need to replenish your wallet; now you rarely needed to go to the bank (once an occasion for dressing up and looking respectable), and bankers' hours ceased to matter. Finally, electronic home banking and online bill payment came along. These days, the old bank building is likely to be a Starbucks.

It's at Provincetown, on the far tip of Cape Cod—the place of which Henry David Thoreau said, "One may stand here and put all of America behind him"—that the cycle of architectural decline and rebirth has turned most tellingly. This was where the Puritans, acting on King James's invitation to love it or leave it, made their first North American landing. By the mid-nineteenth century it was a wealthy boomtown, with a huge fleet of schooners and fine houses, but with the decline of New England fishing and whaling in the latter part of the century it collapsed like a dot-com stock—but left a residue of picturesque buildings ready for eventual upmarket, postindustrial uses. Then, in the early decades of the last century, the artists and writers came to town; an old fish shack on Lewis Wharf was converted into the theater that gave Eugene O'Neill his start, storefronts and homes became galleries, and grand old residences reinvented themselves as bohemian boarding houses. It became the magical, light-filled place that Norman Mailer described in *Tough Guys Don't Dance*.

More recently, in a reverse-flow pilgrimage to the place that held such hope for the Puritans, gay men and women have flocked to Ptown. By purchasing and rehabilitating property, starting businesses, and taking an increasingly assertive role in local politics, they have established a genuine, if modest and imperfect, utopia—a refuge from the blasts of bone-headed bigotry that continue to emanate from Washington, the

Vatican, and whatever rock Pat Robertson lives under. I can't forget the joyful couple I met in Clem and Ursie's seafood shack, as my vacationing family tucked into fried clams and cold beer. The news was out that the ever-civilized Canadians would soon legalize gay marriage, and the two of them were planning a trip to Toronto. As they mugged for their friends' cameras ("For the wedding album," they said) we raised our Red Stripes and wished them well.

The current effort to unseat and replace the Governor of California has flushed a rabble of ratbags that makes Screaming Lord Sutch and the Monster Raving Loony Party look like models of sober rectitude. It has been the year's silly-season story, frothy and diverting as iced cappuccino in the late summer heat. But, in juxtaposition to Howard Dean's emerging presidential campaign, it has also become a vivid parable of the shifting venues of political life—of orators and urban public space, celebrities and twentieth century mass-media space, and grass-roots activists exploring the uses of twenty-first century cyberspace.

This opera buffa was initiated by a wealthy hawker of car alarms, who hired functionaries to go out and collect signatures for a recall petition at a dollar apiece. When he had served his purpose, but had also demonstrated his own unattractiveness as a candidate, he weepingly withdrew from the race—leaving it to a field of 135. The roster of hopefuls includes: a minor comedian who thinks it's whacko funny to smash watermelons, a sometime columnist who specializes in soap-opera marriages and divorces (her own), a thick-necked action movie star who's getting too old to hack it in that genre (even in the age of Botox) and whose last effort required huge injections of advertising dollars to pump it up at the box office, and a porn actress who announced, "I'm just as dignified as Arnold Schwarzenegger, and I can speak English," while displaying an even bigger chest. Apart from the lieutenant governor Cruz Bustamante—a competent, experienced politician who has worked effectively on behalf of the state's appallingly disadvantaged Hispanic population—the most credible is Larry Flynt, publisher of *Hustler*, who bills himself as "the smut peddler who cares." Some of his one-liners aren't bad, and he does have a record of courageously supporting free speech. Anyway, if Citizen Kane and Silvio Berlusconi could use their equally tawdry press empires to launch lunges at political power, why not Citizen Porn?

For those interested in the pathologies of public discourse, the Schwarzenegger campaign has been most instructive. There is a lot of fat-cat money behind it, including Arnie's own, to create newsworthy events and buy media time. It was kicked off with a series of hints and teases to the press, then announced in a carefully scripted appearance on a television talk show. Arnold bin Terminator has obviously learned a lot from Osama about the fascist aestheticization of violence. The trick is to appear powerful by associating yourself with scenes of fiery death and destruction, then to show up on television screens mouthing menacing one-liners—"Death to America," or "You are hasta la vista, baby." It is satisfying to followers who don't want to think, it doesn't leave room for argument, and it saves you the trouble of having to answer questions about actual policies. The relationship of the electronic image to a real human being doesn't much matter, as long as the performance is sufficiently compelling and you can sustain sufficient levels of ambiguity about troublesome questions that might arise.

The gurus of this sort of thing talk a lot about trusted brands, and about expanding power by extending brands from one domain to another. So, for example, Vivendi built a brand selling water, then moved on to entertainment. Similarly, Schwarzenegger's packagers propose to extend the Terminator brand from the pornography of violence—smashing women's heads with urinals, and otherwise stylishly slaughtering people on screen (at last count, several hundred of them)—to fiscal policy and stewardship of the University of California. His handlers are selling him as the killer who cares.

All this would really have gotten Plato's toga in a twist. He thought that a state's citizens should all come together in the agora, face-to-face, to thrash out political issues. ("Citizens," of course, did not include women, slaves, or foreigners—but that is another issue.) If you wanted to advance a cause, you addressed a crowd directly. Similarly, in his *Politics*, Aristotle suggested, "In order to give decisions on matters of justice, and for the purpose of distributing offices of merit, it is necessary that the citizens should know each other and know what kind of people they are." But the trouble with Greek and Roman prescriptions for political authenticity was that they didn't scale. You ran up against the fundamental limits of architecture—specifically, of the agora and the forum. When the size of a community grew beyond 5,000 or so (the limit proposed by Plato in the *Laws*), you couldn't just stand up in a public place, ask your countrymen to lend you their ears, and hope to reach them all. To enable inclusive political discussion and decision-making in today's larger-scale political units—certainly ones the size of California—you can't rely upon old-style bricks and mortar; you have to enlist modern information technology.

The information technologies dominating the California recall election are expensive, one-way, broadcast systems that confer huge advantages on wealthy candidates who can afford access to them, marginalize dissenting voices, and encourage strategies of branding and spin rather than serious, substantive debate. It's all *so* twentieth century. But meanwhile, from isolated Burlington, Vermont, Howard Dean's hot presidential campaign is betting on another, newer technology for scaling up the agora—the Internet. The viral, bottom-up propagation of Web links and email lists supports grass-roots campaigning that is not constrained by distance. Blogs and online forums substitute highly interactive discussion on a large scale for the broadcasting of packaged messages. The efficiency of e-commerce technology enables micro-funding—the financing of a campaign through a large number of small donations collected over a wide area, rather that from large corporate contributions and bigtime donors. And, in a way that would have gratified Plato, Dean has effectively woven the connection to urban public space through a "Sleepless Summer Tour" of rallies in cities across the country, coordinated through Web sites, email, and wireless messaging. He has dramatically entered the forum of the twenty-first century. And, so far in his engagement of the honorable men currently in power, he's making out like Mark Anthony.

Architects have always understood that the possibility of democracy depends upon the availability of spaces for political discourse—and upon the particular ways that those spaces structure discourse. We make our places for politics, then those places make us, if you want to get Churchillian. But it's no longer about sizing the agora or shaping the Houses of Parliament. Maybe, as the parallel political dramas of Schwarzenegger and Dean suggest, it's now about the difference between broadcast mass media and the Internet.

A long time ago, in a galaxy far, far away (or so it seems now) the Internet and electronic commerce were supposed to kill off traditional forms of retail space. It didn't work out that way. But new technologies and business models have transformed the competitive environment for retail spaces, with profound implications for their roles and design—much as the horseless carriage consigned the horse to the recreational and entertainment sector, photography freed painting to assume new forms and cultural functions, and steam power shifted sailing to the harbor on a sunny afternoon.

Here is one success we can chalk up for electronic retailing. In Cambridge, Massachusetts, where I happen to live, lots of two-career professional couples order their everyday groceries online from Peapod. The Web site is efficient, and, of course, you can access it 24/7. The quality is reliable and you can schedule home delivery at convenient times. It is a little more expensive, but not so much so as to make a difference. It makes sense for busy people who don't have time to get to the supermarket during normal opening hours.

At the weekends, though, I see crowds of those same professionals at Formaggio—the fancy local cheese and wine store. They mill around sampling the incredibly expensive artisinal goat cheese from obscure corners of France, selecting figs and olives from seductive displays, and reading the labels of wine bottles from villages you have never heard of. They come for the sensual experience of smelling and tasting, the opportunity to learn about new culinary pleasures from professional foodies, and the chance to socialize with friends over the perfectly ripened Brie. Right now, there are local heirloom tomatoes, in variegated colors, shapes, and flavors that (remember, it's Cambridge) offer a cultural critique of the uniform, industrialized red objects you find on the supermarket shelves. You can't get these things on the Web. A place that is pleasurable and unique is still a powerful attractor, and busy people will devote some of their scarce leisure time to visiting it.

Peapod and Formaggio are both successful food-retailing systems, but it is clear that they do not directly substitute for one another. They offer different attractions, make different demands on our time, and hit our wallets in different ways. And their contrast illustrates some of the key properties of the twenty-first century's new economy of presence. In the digital network era, we continually make choices among different ways of establishing contact and carrying out transactions. Telecommunications technologies now allow us to conduct our business remotely as well as face-to-face; storage technologies enable asynchronous transactions as well as synchronous ones; and the various combinations of local versus remote and synchronous versus asynchronous define our options. If you are a well-behaved homo economicus, you choose, for any particular purpose, the combination that offers you the best available combination of efficiency and pleasure.

The combination traditionally favored for retailing is, of course, that of local synchronous interaction. Over the centuries, this has motivated the architectural and urban arrangements of the market square, the bazaar, the High Street storefront, the downtown department store, the supermarket, the suburban shopping center, the strip mall, the big-box category-killer, and the street vendor's blanket spread with fake Rolexes. These are all places for bringing buyers and sellers face-to-face in the presence of the goods. They continue to work well where direct, personal relationships between buyers and sellers are important, where you need to lay eyes and hands directly on the merchandise, and where they offer an ambience you want to experience. They may exploit their uniqueness and local character, or they may be points of presence for global brands, like Prada, that promise prestige by association to those seen shopping there.

The telephone brought us remote synchronous interaction, the possibility of calling in a pizza order, the shopping channel, the plague of junk sales calls at dinner time, and the word "phony"—which originally applied to smooth-tongued telephone salesmen who relied on the fact that you couldn't look them in the eye. The retail spaces that emerged to accommodate this form of interaction were the call center, its low-rent cousin the boiler-room, and the order fulfillment center. For retailers, these facilities offer efficient access to geographically dispersed markets. From an urban perspective, the crucial consequence is the transfer of retail jobs from their traditional locations to the outer suburbs, rural areas with low labor costs, or even offshore. And from the viewpoint of the customer, remote synchronous commerce shifts the activity of shopping into domestic or workspace and reduces the requirement for physical mobility.

The unattended farm stand, with its honor box to deposit payment for your fruit and vegetable purchases, is a site for local asynchronous interaction. Buyer and seller come to the same place, but they do not have to be there at the same time. In contexts where it would be unwise to rely so completely upon trust, vending machines serve the same purpose. They are not much fun, but they can offer the convenience of a cool drink exactly when and where you need it. And they can provide unsupervised access to goods such as tobacco, alcohol, and contraceptives—which is a problem or an opportunity, depending upon your relationship to structures of authority.

During the 1990s, we saw the sudden rise of remote asynchronous interaction, as enabled by email and the World Wide Web. To conduct retail transactions online, you don't have to go to a store or a vending machine, you don't have to worry about opening hours, and you don't have to wait to get a representative on the phone. Online retail sites, such as Peapod.com and Amazon.com, provide the possibility of shopping wherever and whenever you can get an Internet connection—which is now pretty much anywhere and anytime. From the buyer's viewpoint, shopping becomes a placeless activity. For the sellers, places of business are now server farms, backroom e-commerce centers at locations where labor markets are attractive, and enormous warehouses and distribution centers at nodes in large-scale transportation networks. Instead of talking to their customers, retailers obtain market knowledge by applying software to analyze databases of online transaction records. As entrepreneurs discovered during the dot-com years, this model works particularly well for compact, varied, high-value items like books and electronic gadgets, but it isn't great for dog food.

As it turns out, though, the most profound and provocative outcome of the dot-com era was not the straightforward substitution of online retail sites for physical ones. It was the development of entirely new distribution strategies for certain types of goods. Person-to-person trading sites, such as eBay, created vast, geographically distributed, asynchronous auction houses and flea markets where you could find almost anything that was legal—plus a few things that were not. Book publishers turned to increasingly capable print-on-demand technology, which substituted server space for book warehouses and retail display shelves, and meant that no book need ever go out of print. Meanwhile, Napster and its buccaneering successors forced peer-to-peer online distribution of music and movies onto a greedy and decadent entertainment industry—which responded desperately by trying to criminalize its customers.

As we enter the era of microtechnology and nanotechnology, retail spaces are being invaded by things that think— objects and surfaces that intelligently mediate among customers, the goods on offer, and electronic information. Rem Koolhaas's Prada store in SoHo is an elegant, fetishistic shrine to embedded microprocessor, video display, liquid crystal, and

RF LAN technology of the early 2000s—all now rapidly obsolescing. It is, of course, about branding through the theatrical heightening of everyday experience; there are simpler ways to buy shoes and handbags. At the other end of the chic scale, the mass retailer Wal-Mart recently announced that it would begin deploying billions of RFID (radio frequency identification) tags, embedded in cases and pallets, to further automate their supply chain management processes. Henceforth, store shelves will know when items are removed from them, and checkout counters will know what is passing by them.

The dawning truth, now that the breathlessness of the dot-com bubble is receding into history, is that no established type of retail system ever goes away—though its roles may shift, and wax and wane in importance. As each successive system emerges, it takes its place within the economy of presence, and adds to our options within that economy. At the same time, the endless inventiveness of buyers and sellers produces new hybrid practices, such as making price comparisons on your wireless telephone or PDA while you examine goods in a store. The challenge for architects is to understand how each type of retail space—time-honored or recently invented by some teenage hacker—functions within today's evolving economy of presence, and to discover in it opportunities to renew the ancient, archetypal human experience of going to market.

The surprise hit of the current American television season is *Queer Eye for the Straight Guy*. The Web site blurbs the set-up: "They are the Fab Five: an elite team of gay men dedicated to extolling the simple virtues of style, taste and class. Each week their mission is to transform a style-deficient and culture-deprived straight man from drab to fab." The mise-en-scène goes from dirty socks, sweatshirts, and pizza boxes to SoHo chic and a parting shot of a grateful girlfriend gasping with delight. There are enough layers of irony, reflexivity, and street-smart parody of gender stereotypes to gobsmack a gaggle of queer theorists.

But the RIBA (Royal Institute of British Architects) might take a cue from the RIAA (Recording Industry Association of America) and send out a few subpoenas. Architects have traditionally distributed this sort of culture, and they have a crumbling monopoly to protect. They even invented the taste-and-class makeover genre. To set the record straight, let's query the IP of those Bravo Channel guys.

The story begins, if I'm not mistaken, with that frightfully fab man of letters Giangiorgio Trissino's transformation of a provincial, style-deficient stonemason—maestro Andrea di Pietro. Trissino took charge of this kid from Padua's education, introduced him to the works of Vitruvius, Serlio, and Alberti, and in the 1540s swept him off to Rome, where he encountered the style of the ancients firsthand. And the wide-eyed youngster took note of how Bramante, Raphael, Peruzzi, and all the rest had deployed classical motifs and compositional principles in contemporary projects. Pretty soon, he was the renowned architect *messer* Andrea *Palladio*—a Roman name chosen for him by Trissino.

In 1546, Trissino (like a Philip Johnson of his day, a great promoter of up-and-coming talent) got Palladio the job of wrapping a new, two-story loggia around the drab and unfashionably gothic Palazzo della Ragione in Vicenza. Palladio gave it an up-to-the-minute, 60,000-ducat, Roman-style makeover by facing it with stone *serliane* and renaming it the Basilica. He went from success to success, and in 1570—looking back on a long and illustrious career—published his own illustrated volume of stylistic advice, the *Quattro Libri*. He wrote it, as the Palladio historian Howard Burns has commented, "to educate, to improve general standards of architectural design," and in this he succeeded brilliantly. For generations of Palladio's intellectual heirs, ranging from Inigo Jones and Lord Burlington to Thomas Jefferson, it served as *Italian Eye for the Foreign Guy*.

By the nineteenth century, the wheel of stylistic reincarnation had turned again, and the pointy stuff was back. To plug it, in 1836, Augustus Welby Pugin published *Contrasts; or, A Parallel Between the Noble Edifices of the XIVth and XVth Centuries, and Similar Buildings of the Present Day, &c. &c. &c.* Unlike the

Fab Five, Pugin wasn't into cheerfully disgusted persiflage. He just opened right up with "On comparing the Architectural Works of the present Century with those of the Middle Ages, the wonderful superiority of the latter must strike every attentive observer." Presaging the storyboards for *Queer Eye*, Pugin's volume mostly consisted of paired illustrations comparing the current, culture-deprived urban scene with the exemplar of simple, idyllic virtue it might become. He had a great eye for telling details, and drew them with the venomous glee of an architecturally obsessed Steve Bell. Along with his other fiercely polemical works, *Contrasts* was to function effectively as *Medieval Eye for the Victorian Guy*.

Le Corbusier was gunning for both neo-gothic and neo-classical when he published *Vers Une Architecture* in 1923. He announced (repeatedly) that, "Architecture has nothing to do with the various "styles" . . . they are to architecture what a feather is on a woman's head; it is sometimes pretty, though not always, and never anything more." You've gotta go for the "masterly, correct and magnificent play of masses brought together in light." Furthermore, "THE AMERICAN ENGINEERS OVER-WHELM WITH THEIR CALCULATIONS OUR EXPIRING ARCHITECTURE." He fulminated about "eyes which do not see,"—advising his browbeaten readers to contemplate biplanes, Bugattis, and grain elevators. (He would not have been pleased with the retro moves of today's car designers.) Then, in 1927, he set down his Fab Five points of contrast between the decadent, old-fashioned stuff and the work of the new spirit—*5 points d'une architecture nouvelle*, his shot at *Modernist Eye for the Beaux-Arts Guy*.

A few decades later the revolutionary spirit of the early modernist masters had hardened into a mind-numbing orthodoxy, and the mid-century corporate modernists were producing some undeniably un-fab stinkers. Robert Venturi was there to proclaim the awfulness of all this, and to propose a makeover. To "less is more," he famously retorted, "less is a bore." To those put out by the messiness of the everyday, he responded, "Is not Main Street almost all right?" As he has summarized: "We were calling for an architecture that promotes richness and ambiguity over unity and clarity, contradiction and redundancy over harmony and simplicity." In 1966 he put it all together in *Complexity and Contradiction in Architecture*—his extraordinary excursion into *Postmodern Irony for the Sixties Guy*.

From then on, it wasn't so much the eye as the gaze. From successive waves of post-(fill in the blank) discourse, architectural theorists and critics have learned to watch out for the gaze of power, the gaze of desire, the objectifying gaze, the gaze of whatever might turn out to be troublesome. And critically resistant eye for an eye—*Feminist Eye for the Unreconstructed Guy, Postcolonial Eye for the Orientalist Guy*, plus endless variants on these sorts of themes—has become a vigorous academic industry. We are now much less innocent about the complexities of cultural identity and the subtle intertwining of culture and power. For all its gestures at hip boundary bending, *Queer Eye* is about nostalgic yearning for a simpler time, an era in which confident arbiters of style and taste could dispense authoritative, universal answers.

When New Year's Eve rolls around again, New York's Times Square will, as usual, be on all our television screens. But this time, as the ball drops at midnight, forget about the freezing revelers and focus instead on the surrounding urban scenery. You will discover a provocative new relationship of urban space, digital information, and light.

The groundwork for this was laid early last century. When Sergei Eisenstein first encountered New York in the 1920s, he was astonished by the city's dematerialization at dusk. As he recalled in *The Film Sense*, "All sense of perspective and realistic depth is washed away by a nocturnal sea of electric advertising. Far and near, small (in the foreground) and large (in the background), soaring aloft and dying away, racing and circling, bursting and vanishing—these lights tend to abolish all sense of real space, finally melting into a single plane of colored light points and neon lines moving over a surface of black velvet sky."

Now you can program these glowing points. It is easy enough, with some hardware from Radio Shack, to hook a lightbulb up to your laptop computer. Then you can switch it on and off under software control. More interestingly, you can instruct it to pulse at different paces and with different rhythms, or to blink out messages in binary code. If you introduce a dimmer into the circuit you can begin to play not only with on and off states, but also with varying intensities. You have the beginnings of what electronic culture theorists (updating Eisenstein for the digital era) would call a time-based expressive medium.

For a graphic designer, the obvious next step is to arrange individually controllable light sources on a surface. This gives you a simple computer graphics display—as signage designers in Las Vegas and along Broadway long ago discovered. Arrange millions of such programmable sources in a rectangular grid and you get the now-familiar raster display screen—at any scale from that of your camera phone to that of the huge video displays in sports stadiums. But, if you are an architect, you might think instead of deploying programmable points in three-dimensional space. In other words, the composition of mass and surface converges with computer animation.

Several technologies have come together to create this emerging hybrid. Advances in solid-state lighting technologies have enabled the fabrication of very large assemblages of reliable, controllable light sources that can be wrapped onto just about any sort of surface. The miniaturization of electronics has allowed the association of control circuitry with each individual light. Wireless technology can provide computer control without running cables to every one of these. You can give each glowing point a network address and exert control by sending packets of bits (even email messages) to it. With all this, the traditional distinctions between architectural lighting design and computer graphics are beginning to disappear. Anything that lights up can be treated as an addressable, programmable pixel.

Programmable LED displays have, in the last few years, covered more and more of the surfaces surrounding Times Square, so that they now play the major role in defining the space—particularly at night. But the whole thing hasn't yet come together in a fully convincing way. Instead, the uses of the new medium remain in an archaic, skeuomorphic phase— much like that of marble Greek temples that imitated the forms and details of their wooden predecessors, or bronze axes that replicated the leather binding patterns of wood-handled stone weapons. We are still seeing horseless carriage, wireless telegraph thinking.

Some of the first LED surfaces in Times Square directly appropriated the form of the billboard—merely substituting animated images for static ones. Others presented themselves as friezes, with text in lights, scrolling horizontally instead of being chiseled in stone. Theater marquees were soon being handled in the same way, and Jenny Holzer seized on the form for her own sly purposes. On the NASDAQ building, the LED display surface was wrapped into a half-cylinder to define the corner. In an obvious but surprisingly effective substitution, all the spandrel panels of the curtain wall on the Lehman Brothers building became sheets of LED. And, on those New Year's Eve television screens, pixels now represent pixels—to be played back into the space, on giant displays, in an endless recursion.

Like murals in perspective, videos and three-dimensional animations displayed on these surfaces create illusory depth. But they do so dynamically, so that the shape and scale of Times Square now seems to transform unceasingly and at eye-popping speed—specially since the editing is mostly bang-bang MTV-style. The cinematic moves of horizontally and vertically panning or scrolling reinforce the continuity of the architectural surfaces, but zooming and high-speed motion out of the picture plane shatter them. Chunks of display are programmed individually, like the screens of personal computers, so that the overall effect is one of juxtaposed fragments; there is, as yet, very little exploration of the potential for formal and thematic unity across complete buildings or entire urban spaces. At the moment, it is all raw energy and excitement without much finesse, like early rock and roll.

You can argue, of course, that architecture has always been about animated surface—classical effects of shade and shadow as sun and clouds move (What are moldings for, after all?), Barcelona Pavilion effects of reflection and transparency created by glass, metal, and machine-polished surface, and subtle combinations of the two, as at L.A.'s new Disney Concert Hall. In a sense, too, buildings have been computing visual effects all along—much like elaborate sundials, or optical instruments, with their programming contained in their geometry. Now, though, we can separate the software of architectural dynamics from the hardware, execute this software at high speed on inexpensive digital devices, and reprogram effects whenever we like.

Post-whatever media theory doesn't provide much help to designers who want to figure all this out. We need some unregenerate high modernists who are prepared to probe the essential nature of the new medium, and rigorously explore its characteristic expressive possibilities—like Eisenstein with film, Brecht with radio, Corb with reinforced concrete, or Kahn with radically reimagined bricks. What does a pixel want to be?

For the last time, I'm writing this column on my Macintosh G4 titanium laptop. When it came into my life a couple of years ago, it was elegant, desirable, and the right sort of arm candy to be seen with in fashionable places. But those days have gone. It's now scratched and scuffed from hard use, and the surface coating has chipped off at the corners. Faithless as an aging rock star, I'm about to dump this raddled former beauty for the latest, perkiest, most radiantly unblemished newcomer—this time in brushed aluminum alloy.

Apple's choice of "natural" metal surfaces for its new line of PowerBooks is a consumer electronics reprise of a characteristic late modernist, Herzog and de Meuron theme—the dramatic, beautifully rendered revelation of traditional material properties and fabrication effects in contexts where we have learned to expect paint, plastics, and other elaborately synthetic industrial products. It's like the stainless steel DeLorean challenging the familiar Detroit paint job, or sashimi-smitten chefs scorning sauces and glazes. Meanwhile, though, the most innovative current materials research is suggesting a radically different direction—that of adventurously exploiting micro-fabrication techniques and nanotechnology to provide thin surface layers with surprising new functions.

It's a story that began in 1959 with a lecture entitled "There's Plenty of Room at the Bottom" by the irrepressibly imaginative Richard Feynman. In it, he proposed the atom-by-atom construction of structures and devices with key dimensions measured in billionths of a meter, and went on to suggest some sensational uses, such as the replacement of surgical suites by tiny, robotic heart surgeons that worked from the inside of blood vessels like tunnel repair workers. In the decades since, researchers have converged on Feynman's vision from two directions. From the top down, technologies for fabrication of computer chips and MEMS (microelectromechanical systems) have achieved finer and finer resolution, and are heading for nanoscale. From the bottom up, chemists, materials scientists, and guys with lasers and scanning tunneling microscopes have learned to synthesize buckyballs (buckminsterfullerene, clusters of carbon atoms arranged in hollow spheres instead of graphite's sliding sheets), carbon nanotubes, and other interesting and potentially useful nanostructures. Computer scientists and theoretical biologists (the difference is disappearing) have contributed some interesting ideas about error correction and self-replication in the assembly of large and complex structures from small pieces. Today, the venture capitalists are reading business plans for nanotechnology startups and Prince Charles is having nightmares not just about modernist concrete, but about runaway, self-replicating gray goo.

For architects, nanostructures and nanodevices become particularly interesting when you embed lots of them in some substrate, like particles of pigment in layers of paint. You can engineer them to perform increasingly complex functions, and thus make the surfaces of buildings do things they could never do before. Take self-cleaning, for example. Instead of scrubbing surfaces from the outside, with buckets and mops in the time-honored way, you can provide armies of nanoscale automatic cleaners that—like Feynman's nanorobot surgeons—do it from the inside. These can take the form of titanium dioxide particles. When pieces of nasty organic stuff encounter them, in the presence of ultraviolet light, a photocatalytic reaction takes place, and the bonds holding the organic molecules together break down. The guck simply falls apart and gets washed away in the next rain.

Particles of electronic ink, such as those supplied by E Ink of Cambridge, Massachusetts, are even more interesting. These are microcapsules, with about the diameter of a human hair, filled with a mixture of positively charged white particles and negatively charged black particles suspended in a clear fluid. A negative electric field pulls the white particles to the top, and a positive field has the reverse effect. (Think of it as painting from the inside of the canvas.) Electronic ink of this sort can be printed on to just about any kind of surface, and controlled by integrated circuitry to create dynamic displays—video on paper, ceramics, cloth, and plastics. As it becomes more robust and capable, and as its cost drops, it will enable animated murals and wallpaper. Signage will become integral and continuous with the surface on which it is mounted, and will lie dormant and invisible until it is electronically activated. There will be new opportunities for both exuberant decoration and the most austere minimalism.

Technologies for varying the transparency of glass have been around for a while, and have been used to create electronic window shades, but the design possibilities expand excitingly when miniaturized electronic components add the possibility of fine-grained control. Imagine, for example, a frit pattern that can appear, disappear, and vary in scale and opacity. And stained glass is now being reinvented for the digital era. In a system under development by Carlo Ratti at the MIT Media Laboratory, tiny squares of transparency-varying film become pixels in window-sized see-through displays.

Textiles, too, are becoming programmable. In other Media Laboratory projects, woven and embroidered fabrics contain smart thread structures that can serve as sensors, mechanical actuators that shorten and lengthen, and color-varying lines, patches, or pixel arrays. One current project is exploring the possibility of couches with memories; when you sit on them, you leave visible traces that slowly fade away. The fabric surfaces thus present themselves as continually transforming overlays of digital shadows.

Some of the most dramatic recent developments have been in lighting. Here, increasingly tiny and efficient solid-state devices—particularly LEDs, light-emitting diodes—are challenging the bulky glass spheres and tubes that we have known for so long. LEDs can vary their intensities and colors. They can readily be embedded in strips of tape, or arrayed on surfaces. These arrays can be dense or sparse, and on opaque, transparent, or optically variable substrates to provide a huge variety of effects. Lighting is becoming a function of surfaces rather than of discrete fixtures, and the difference between lighting and information display systems is rapidly vanishing.

It now seems clear that the miracle material of the future will be a complex, fine-grained composite. It will consist of a substrate providing electrical power and digital networking, together with varying mixes of specialized, embedded particles that provide sensing capability, memory and processing power, communication, mechanical actuation, and controlled variation in optical, thermal, and acoustic properties. It will suck into the wallboard many of the current functions of lights, televisions and computer monitors, computing and communication devices, cleaning systems, thermostats, and interior climate control systems. Its functionality will only be skin-deep, but that will be enough.

15 | The Wireless Groves

Once, you could tell engineering students by their slide rules and architecture students by their drafting instruments. These days, the students in my classes carry wireless laptop computers instead of notepads, pencils, and the traditional emblems of their specializations. The shift to standardized, miniaturized, networked electronics marks a revolutionary change in lecture hall and seminar room dynamics, but not one that that has happened overnight. It has emerged, in stages, over decades.

At Yale in the 1960s, where I first practiced my trade as a teacher, the mainframe computers of the day were huge, expensive, and needy. So the campus computer center was the sole point of presence of a scarce and precious resource—much like a traditional village well. If you worked with a computer, you didn't want to be too far from the center, since you had to lug boxes of punch cards back and forth. It wasn't so different from carrying water in a jar on your head. But in the decades since, computers have become progressively more numerous and less expensive, and at each stage in their evolution towards ubiquity they have enabled new types of learning communities and creative teams.

The computer center was not a very pleasant place—freezingly air-conditioned as the big hot machines required, noisy, and industrially lit—but it had its compensations. Like the village well, it generated a lively public space in the surrounding area. You could rely upon seeing other computer users there, and it was a place to *be* seen. As you waited for your job to process, you could socialize, and exchange news and gossip. Most importantly, it concentrated the specialized expertise of an intellectual community, and became a place of intense, round the clock, peer-to-peer learning. You could always find someone to help you with the finer points of Fortran syntax, explain the meaning of an arcane error message, or trace back through a hexadecimal dump to locate a problem. After too much time there, of course, its isolation and specificity did make you want to get out more, and to engage the wider life of the university.

The more specialized computer laboratories that emerged to pursue pioneering research in computer graphics, artificial intelligence, and the like, functioned in much the same way—but even more intensely. To facilitate peering at the faint displays of cathode ray tube terminals, the lighting was dimmer. And a glowing computer, like a shrine with votive candles, typically occupied the center of the workspace. The communities that inhabited these places were smaller and more privileged, and they saw themselves as the repositories of advanced, unique, sometimes even dangerous knowledge. The style of learning that prevailed was, ironically enough, an ancient one—that of the craft workshop and the design atelier. You had to earn your status as an initiate and an insider, and you had to maintain it by performing virtuoso feats. It was the beginning of the hacker culture, and of institutions like the MIT Media Laboratory.

When I first saw the Arpanet sputtering into life at UCLA, I knew that all this would eventually change. The function of any network is to *distribute* points of presence of some resource, and thus to enable the emergence of new spatial and social patterns. But the consequences are mixed. If you provide a village with a piped water supply system, you certainly allow it to spread out along the pipelines, and you produce greater convenience by shifting the access points into private space, but you destroy the capacity of the old well to sustain a social focus. Similarly, if you replace the family hearth with networks of electric lights and hot water radiators, you make more of your domestic space useable on cold, dark nights, and you allow the separation of incompatible activities, but you lose a powerful way of bringing the family regularly together within a small circle of warmth and light. And sure enough, as the Arpanet evolved into the global Internet, as Ethernet and inexpensive personal computers came along, and as Web servers and clients proliferated, the associated learning communities transformed as well.

When network jacks and computer workstations began to multiply and distribute themselves across campuses, they also encouraged fragmentation and privatization of work areas. If you had convenient access in your office or dormitory room, you had little motivation to come out and work in more public areas, and your colleagues saw less of you. Furthermore, there were growing tensions between traditional loyalties to local, spatial communities and emerging allegiances to far-flung, online communities of interest. But there were also opportunities for some positive spatial engineering. At the Harvard Design School in the 1980s, I convinced my dean to shut down the basement laboratories that had hitherto ghettoized computational work, and to equip each student desk in the design studio spaces with a network drop and a personal computer. It was like mixing chemicals and waiting for a reaction. The cultures of design and computation productively came together, and the place hasn't been the same since.

Today, my MIT students have laptop computers that provide wireless Internet access throughout the campus and beyond. Mobility means that computers no longer establish fixed, specialized sites of learning. Instead, they enhance the potential of *every* sort of space to support intellectual activity, and in doing so, they encourage new, fluid, and potentially creative combinations of research and scholarly practices. The students are discovering that a laptop-friendly café table is the right sort of place for a brainstorming session over a sandwich, that a shady spot under a tree serves nicely as a quiet, private place to hack code on a sunny day, and that the couch by the large-format plotter is a convenient place to answer email while keeping an eye out for your poster in the print queue. So there is diminishing need on campus for formally designated work areas populated with fixed desktop computers, and growing demand for pleasant, flexible spaces that offer a variety of characters and atmospheres, and that can informally be appropriated as needed.

In the class I'm teaching right now—which happens to focus upon radically rethinking the automobile and designing a concept car—my students and I are as peripatetic as Socrates and his companions strolling among the groves. We meet when and where it suits our current purposes, and our meetings are coordinated on the fly by email and instant messaging. We have our wireless computers, augmented by video cameras, projectors, and conferencing to remote participants as necessary. Whenever some topic emerges in the course of conversation, a couple of the students will instantly Google it and immediately introduce any interesting results into the discussion. As we accumulate data, examples, references, Web pointers, ideas, sketches, CAD models, and other material relevant to our interests, we record it all in a blog-like Web site that represents our small community's evolving, jointly-constructed intellectual capital— accessible to any of us, at any time, from anywhere in the world. We combine the focus and intensity of the atelier with ongoing, vigorous utilization of the wide and varied opportunities offered by our physical and online environments.

This sort of creative practice may not look very disciplined, and it may horrify those who still see teaching as the structured, authoritative dispensation of knowledge, but it is thrillingly intense, and it enables us to make astonishingly rapid progress. It works, and I'm prepared to bet that it will become a prevailing pattern for learning communities and creative teams in the twenty-first century.

The singing demographer, Frank Sinatra, famously observed of New York, New York, "If I can make it there, I'll make it anywhere." The city that never sleeps is a powerful talent magnet, a migration mecca for go-getting youngsters intent on melting away those little town blues. The 2000 U.S. Census confirmed that the ongoing flow of talent favored a few such fortunate cities. And the *Washington Post* recently reported: "In a Darwinian fight for survival, American cities are scheming to steal each other's young. They want ambitious young people with graduate degrees in such fields as genome science, bioinformatics and entrepreneurial management." In today's knowledge-based, creative economy, well-trained, up-to-date talent is the most crucial, sought-after resource.

New York, Los Angeles, and Chicago continue to attract healthy shares of up-market brainpower, but it is among the mid-sized cities that the cutthroat competition occurs. Austin, Atlanta, Boston, Denver, Minneapolis, San Diego, San Francisco, Seattle, Washington D.C., and Raleigh/Durham currently head the list of brain-gain cities. On the whole, the smart kids would rather be there than in Philadelphia—though the City of Brotherly Love is currently doing better than it used to. The bottom tier of brain-drain cities features Baltimore, Buffalo, Cleveland, Detroit, Hartford, Milwaukee, Miami, Newark, Pittsburgh, St. Louis, and Stockton/Lodi.

Mostly, this isn't hard to figure out—particularly if you have ever visited Stockton. The brain-gainers are generally prettier places than the brain-drainers, with pleasant climates and high quality of life. They have excellent universities and cultural institutions (though this does not always distinguish them from their rivals), and reputations for tolerance and diversity. And they have the upper hand in an accelerating, winner-take-all game, since the presence of successful and interesting people is a strong attraction to other successful and interesting people.

At the international level, the intellectual history of the twentieth century might well be told as a tale of talent migrations—featuring the vagabond shoes of Viennese architects moving to Los Angeles; American writers to Paris; European physicists to Princeton, Chicago, and Los Alamos; Barry McKenzie to London; Indian engineers to Silicon Valley; and post-Soviet mathematicians (who have quickly figured out capitalism) to whichever Western universities bid highest. In a globalizing world with the big payoffs coming from the knowledge-based, creative end of the economy, a city's economic success increasingly depends upon joining the elite of international brain-gainers.

Nowhere is this truer than in Singapore. The tiny island city-state has virtually no natural resources or agriculture; it has to import water, and even sand for land reclamation. Due to its strategic location it remains an important shipping and air transportation center, but that is not a sufficient base to sustain a high standard of living. Until recently it was a successful center for electronics and other high-end manufacturing, but it is now increasingly difficult to compete with China in that game. The best hope for the future is to become a vibrant center for research, education, professional services to the region, technological innovation and design, and the creative industries. Singapore's economic planners have responded with policy initiatives to encourage these sectors, investment in education and research (including a vast new technological campus currently under design by Fumihiko Maki), and development—by the Jurong Town Corporation—of a new type of new town. This town is named (perhaps it is better to say branded) One North, since it is just one degree north of the equator.

One North is a place to watch: it is innovative in its program, ambitious in its urban design, and adventurous in its architectural realization. It is conceived of as a global talent hub where, as the press releases put it, "A critical mass of talents, entrepreneurs, scientists and researchers can congregate, exchange ideas and interact." Research and development laboratories and creative production facilities form the core of the project, but it sets itself apart from traditional research parks and technopoles by creating a self-contained, live-work environment that emphasizes exceptionally high quality of life, and provides public spaces designed to encourage intellectual interaction. The site is a beautiful high ridge adjacent to the National University of Singapore, and the master plan—the outcome of an international competition—is by Zaha Hadid. It features a spine of green public space (which will quickly become lush in Singapore's tropical climate), and high-density massing of buildings around an irregular grid of narrow shaded streets.

The first stages of the project, consisting of a biotech research cluster known as Biopolis, and an art-oriented, live-work center at Chip Bee Gardens, are now operational. The next stage, named Fusionopolis, has been designed by Kisho Kurokawa. It is a double-skinned, mixed-use highrise, containing offices and research facilities, residences, sky gardens, retail and food facilities, and public spaces. The first of One North's public spaces—an up-market, air-conditioned version of Singapore's traditional hawker food markets, known as Makan Sutra (Soul Food)—has been an instant hit.

Can such elements and policies become the stuff of true twenty-first century communities? Or will they just produce corporate compounds at busy nodes in global networks—larger versions of international airline lounges, with slightly less transient populations? Clearly this depends upon the successful integration of these places with larger social and cultural contexts, and the jury is still out on that. J. G. Ballard has played out a hairraising, black-humored version of the downside scenario in *Super-Cannes*. He very plausibly conjures up Eden-Olympia— "the newest of the new France, the latest of the development zones that had begun with Sophia-Antipolis and would soon turn Provence into Europe's Silicon Valley." According to the bemused English protagonist (who seems a bit shaky on his Sunday supplement architectural references) it is "a vision of glass and titanium straight from the drawing boards of Richard Neutra and Frank Gehry, but softened by landscaped parks and artificial lakes, a humane version of Corbusier's radiant city." The planners of this Paradise, though, had neglected to allow for the inevitable Ballardian serpent—the potent combination of anomie with privilege and desire under the Mediterranean sun—and it soon emerges that Eden-Olympia's international elite of administrators, *énarques*, and scientific entrepreneurs is industriously occupying itself with sex, drugs, and recreational crime. It all ends badly, of course. As we take leave of the hero, his heroin-addicted wife has been acting out teenage hooker fantasies in the back seat of a Mercedes, his mistress has just come to a particularly sticky end in the bedroom of her seaside apartment, and he's about to go postal with a pump-action shotgun.

But, if talent magnet developments can get the formula right, they will probably become key to urban competitiveness in the twenty-first century. Old Blue Eyes himself left us the marketing template: "Start spreading the news, I'm leaving today. I want to be a part of it—(fill in the blank)."

It's hard to imagine Mies van der Rohe in sneakers. He created big, black, shiny office towers for men—like himself—wearing big, black, shiny shoes. If there's any *geist* in a *zeit* at all, it seems to show up in an uncanny connection between footwear fashions and architecture.

You can see this in the relationship of pointy medieval shoes to pointed gothic architecture (though goth shoes are now, of course, something quite different); Birkenstock sandals to the mellow, woodsy, sixties forms of Sea Ranch; R. M. Williams elastic-sided work boots to Glenn Murcutt's minimalist bush houses; and blobby Air Jordans—already retro by the time architects caught up—with the fashionably blobby buildings of the early 00s. When the new design for the Freedom Tower at the World Trade Center site was recently unveiled, the shoe linkage was obvious; we were seeing the upturned heel of a Manolo Blahnik. It looked as if David Childs and Daniel Libeskind had found the *parti* beside the bed of one of those *Sex and the City* girls.

If you consider the structural logic, it isn't surprising. Both Manolo spikes and world's-tallest-building candidates depend for their dramatic effect upon breathtakingly excessive height combined with improbable slenderness. There is a lot of vertical load, which can punch heels through floor covering and tower footings through bedrock if the bearing surface is too small, but the real structural issue is lateral loading. These engineering wonders cantilever from their attachment points, creating the danger of bending and snapping under wind loading or the eccentricities introduced by a wobbly gait. In both cases, the most elegant answer is a form that tapers prettily from a broad base to a tiny tip.

Between the base and the tip, so long as you maintain adequate dimensions at each level, there is a good deal of freedom to sculpt and texture the surface. Blahnik has always been astonishingly, joyously inventive with slinkily flowing lines, bright colors, and polychrome patterns. Similarly, over the decades, New York architects have gone from the stepped profiles of early twentieth century skyscrapers to the mid-century modernist severity of the original World Trade Center towers, and most recently to sleek, shoe-designer twirls and curves. The Freedom Tower's floor plate is a lozenge that rotates and shrinks as it ascends 70 stories, producing a smoothly warped shape on the skyline that cleverly slims down the bulk of 2.6 million square feet of office space, and would not be out of place in patent leather. The torqued floor plate motif has an immediate (if somewhat stubbier) precedent in Frank Gehry's Neue Zollhof office towers in Düsseldorf, and in a recent Gehry design for a vodka bottle—yes, I know, vodka with a twist!

You don't get to the symbolic 1776 feet specified by Libeskind's competition-winning master plan with 70 stories, and beyond about 70 stories—as Childs no doubt calculated—adding office floors makes little economic sense, so something had to be done to fill the gap. A 400-foot lattice structure, containing wind turbines, gets part of the way. I would be surprised if building a vertical wind farm on a Manhattan rooftop turned out to be an optimal allocation of energy production resources, but at least it's a green gesture in place of the sky gardens that Libeskind had initially proposed. And the return on investment may look a bit better if it's calculated in karma; the *Village Voice* has proposed that the turbines could concurrently serve as Tibetan prayer cylinders, silently cycling through mantras for Wall Street.

Right on top, at one corner, is a narrow spike with roughly the aspect—as tabloid columnists have been all-too-eager to point out—of one of those plastic martini toothpicks. But your actual symbolic mileage may vary, of course, according to your own characteristic habits of cultural reference. An excess of religiosity may prompt readings as a spire or minaret—perhaps serving to hedge the bet on Buddhism below. Aficionados of New York architectural history will, no doubt, detect a gesture of homage to the dirigible mooring mast that tops out the Empire State Building. If you are nostalgic for the golden days of mass media (before cable and the Internet) you will remember the RKO Radio Pictures logo, and see an opportunity for a television transmission tower. If your mind is stocked with recently fashionable but now past-sell-date architectural images and rhetoric, you will recognize it as a sharply edgy shard.

Mostly, though, it just does the job of climbing the remaining 276 feet to 1776.

Finally, the effect of all this vertiginous symbol-mongering is sharpened through contrast with the cluster of lesser towers proposed for the remainder of the site. These are shorter, chunkier, and less flamboyant—the heels, perhaps, of the sensible Kenneth Cole or Nine West pumps favored by junior stock analysts in black business suits.

The problem that this project faces is the classic one of architectural semiotics—as so elegantly formulated, long ago, by Roland Barthes in *Mythologies*. Designers can *declare* the association of some narrative with the forms they produce, as the architects have attempted to do here, but they are not particularly privileged actors in the process of establishing meaning, and their desired associations will not necessarily stick. It is especially tough when they are attempting the unlikely task of projecting a downtown commercial office development as a global icon of political freedom. The meaning will continually be contested and reshaped as the forms take their place in the sign-system of popular culture, and are acted upon by the mechanisms of advertising, campaigning, critical discussion, and tendentious appropriation for rhetorical purposes—the sort of tactic that is currently being pursued, for example, in attack commercials characterizing Howard Dean's presidential campaign as a tax-hiking, government-expanding, latté-drinking, sushi-eating, Volvo-driving, *New York Times*-reading, body-piercing, Hollywood-loving, left-wing freak show that should go back to Vermont where it belongs.

Try a thought experiment. If you can keep your mind firmly fixed upon the great ideals of the American Revolution, you can perhaps read the Freedom Tower, with its upraised arm, as a noble gesture of solidarity with the Statue of Liberty across the water. If you can put yourself in the shoes of a more cynical, *New York Post*-reading, basketball-following Brooklynite, you might think of a really tall Knicks center hailing a cab. And, if you take it as an expression of the Bush-*bis* era's *zeitgeist*—characterized by crude jingoism, big lies about weapons of mass destruction, demonization of ethnic and religious groups (instead of a yellow star, you get your name on an airport watch list), and contempt for civil liberties—you might recognize a fascist salute.

A neutron walks into the fashionable Miracle of Science bar near MIT, orders a Sam Adams, and opens up his wallet to pay. "For you," says the bartender, "no charge!"

That's nerd humor, and a lot of it surfaces around MIT on April Fool's Day. One of its obvious social functions, much like a secret handshake, is to confirm membership of an intellectual elite—to say, I'm smart enough to know what a neutron is. And so, if you get it, are you. (How can I be so sure of this? I don't have data, but I just lost an electron. I'm positive.) Simultaneously, with the logic-defying logic of all good gags, it subverts itself by implicitly ridiculing the preoccupations and values of that elite and expressing resistance to the environment it has created. If you ask undergraduate jokesters what they *really* mean by their discourse of nerd humor, they mostly respond with the slogan IHTFP—"I hate this place," squished to a Pentagon-style acronym and garnished with an expletive. You can take this as a crisp, concise, American formulation of what Henri Lefebvre, Guy Debord, and the Situationists were trying to say about Paris in the 1960s.

The Situationists, bless them, have now passed into cultural history. You can read about *la misère en milieu étudiant*, the Scandinavian Institute for Comparative Vandalism, "Beneath the cobblestones the beach," and the famous tactics of the *dérive*, *détournement*, and *co-ritus* in dense academic treatises. MIT's nerds have never felt the need to frame their jokes and pranks with French-style theoretical apparatus, but they do have a characteristic tactic of their own—the hack. The best hacks are cleverly engineered, site-specific, guerilla interventions that make a provocative point but aren't destructive or dangerous. Unlike hard-core Situationists, who wanted to provoke genuine outrage, true hackers would never consider stunts like absconding with the severed head of Copenhagen's Little Mermaid.

The traces of an early, classic hack are still visible on the Massachusetts Avenue Bridge crossing the Charles River by the MIT campus. In 1958, a five-foot-seven-inch undergraduate named Oliver Reed Smoot was laid out end to end across the bridge to measure its considerable length. It came to 364.4 smoots plus one ear. In good laboratory fashion, the research team marked each smoot with a painted line, and every tenth smoot with a number. When the bridge was rebuilt and resurfaced a few years ago, the smoot marks were carefully replaced— some say because the Cambridge police wanted them to indicate precise locations in accident reports, and some that the Cambridge Historic Society had classified them as cultural patrimony.

The most brilliantly engineered hack was a large, MIT-labeled weather balloon that suddenly rose up out of the turf and inflated itself during a Harvard-Yale football game in 1982. For the same game, hackers surreptitiously switched placards that were meant to spell "Beat Yale" when held up by Harvard supporters. Instead, when the placards were raised, they turned out to spell "MIT"—impudently reminding the assembled fans of a place that, famously, scorns big-time college football.

Many hacks have appropriated the MIT dome as their site. In the 1980s a phone booth was erected at the very top, and when a campus patrolman approached to check it out, the phone rang. A police cruiser was placed there in 1994, complete with a sleeping officer clutching a cup of coffee and a large bag of Dunkin' Donuts. Last December, to celebrate the centenary of flight, a beautiful, full-scale replica of the Wright Flyer appeared at the apex—attracting, fittingly enough, the attention of numerous news helicopters.

Like the Situationists, the perpetrators of these hacks favored iconic public spaces and important public events for their interventions. But, in the early days of information technology, the culture of hacking also spread to MIT's computer laboratories. The young programmers and electrical engineers who frequented these places were proud of their esoteric knowledge and eager to exercise it by making information systems do unexpected and disconcerting things. Long before the days of instant text messaging, for example, Joseph Weizenbaum wrote a computer program called Eliza that conversed with you over a network. It could often con you into thinking that there was a human at the other end of the line, but it actually had no intelligence at all. It was just a bag of programming tricks—a clever hack. Like many early computer hacks, it proved to have legs. The descendents of Eliza are everywhere in the online world today, and we are usually none the wiser.

It was inevitable, I suppose, that hacker culture would spread to wherever networks reached, and that it would lose its Edenic innocence in the process. Today, as we all know to our cost, the serpent got to cyberspace. It is infested with malicious hackers who unleash viruses, worms, and denial-of-service attacks, or remotely take over your computer to surreptitiously store their porn libraries. This doesn't even take a lot of skill. Unless you have bulletproof virus protection software on your computer, there is a pretty good chance that some alienated Bulgarian teenager with a rudimentary knowledge of scripting, an ancient PC, and a dial-up modem will wipe out your hard disk as an April Fool prank.

But the apotheosis of hacking is yet to come. As networked intelligence is increasingly embedded in domestic appliances, automobiles, traffic lights, airplanes and air traffic control systems, telephones, architectural lighting systems, HVAC systems, card-key access systems, portable and wearable devices, and even electronic prosthetics, all of these things are becoming subject to remote hacking. A kid in Katmandu might lock you out of your house and car, switch off your lights, and pipe Abba's greatest hits into your hearing aid at top volume. There will be increasingly sophisticated security systems, of course, but these will not be impregnable—not for long, anyway.

The globalized, ubiquitously networked, electronically intelligent world opens up exciting new design possibilities, and has the potential to bring us extraordinary benefits. It also provides unprecedented ways to carry messages from the disregarded margins to the very centers of power and privilege. We had better be listening carefully. The less pleasant among those messages will be saying, in resourcefully destructive ways, IHTFP.

Since the days of Captain Cook, uninvited visitors to the South Pacific islands have introduced the locals to venereal disease, radioactive contamination, and Sunday school. They have also created a fascinating but little-studied building type—the artist's house in paradise. The remnants of one of the most celebrated works in this genre, Paul Gauguin's House of Pleasure on the island of Hiva Oa in the Marquesas, are currently on display in the wonderful *Gauguin Tahiti* hundredth-anniversary exhibit that is now showing at the Boston Museum of Fine Arts, after it was a huge hit at the Grand Palais in Paris last fall. It invites us to reflect on the architecture of exile, escape, and alluring otherness—the stuff that beach timeshares and Club Meds are now made of.

Reliable scholarship on the colonial architecture of the South Pacific, the tradition within which these artists' houses fall, is hard to come by. (I exclude the suggestive but dubious evidence of the décor in Polynesian restaurants offering pu-pu platters and rum drinks with little umbrellas in them.) But, as far as I can tell, the characteristic South Seas house style originated in a fusion of indigenous materials and *fale* forms with the colonial bungalow type and whatever happened to arrive on passing ships. Jack London got the resulting bricollage just about right in his 1909 story "The House of Mapuhi," when he described an ambitious and newly wealthy islander's dream of an up-to-date residence like those of the missionaries and traders: "It must have a roof of galvanized iron and an octagon-drop-clock. It must be six fathoms long with a porch all around. A big room must be in the center, with a round table in the middle of it and the octagon-drop-clock on the wall. There must be four bedrooms, two on each side of the big room, and in each bedroom must be an iron bed, two chairs, and a washstand. And back of the house must be a kitchen, a good kitchen, with pots and pans and a stove."

For turn-of-the-century writers and artists attracted to the Pacific, construction of a remote island home often served as a desperate act of personal re-imagination and a last shot at some sort of redemption. The terminally sickly Scotsman Robert Louis Stevenson built himself a house near Apia, on the Samoan island of Upolu, and there rewrote himself as Tusitala, teller of tales. The large, airy building, set high on a jungle hillside, had gracious verandahs, a pleasant place to work, and live-in help wearing Royal Stuart tartan *lava lavas*. It served, in effect, as the set for a pre-TV reality show—a lived narrative that emerged not in episodic video format, but as a stream of texts, dispatched by ships on the Sydney-to-San Francisco run, that became *Vailima Letters, Vailima Prayers,* and other books of the prolific Stevenson's last years. The show wrapped up with one of the master storyteller's carefully crafted endings. When the star suddenly died of a cerebral hemorrhage, after four years on the set, the local chiefs worked through the night to cut a path for his coffin up the slopes of nearby Mount Vaea. If you scramble in their tracks today, you come upon a whitewashed grave inscribed, "Here he lies where he long'd to be; home is the sailor, home from the sea, and the hunter home from the hill."

Ted Banfield, known to his once-numerous readers as Beachcomber, was more modest. In the 1890s—overworked and sick to the point of breakdown—he fled the life of a Townsville newspaperman for isolated Dunk Island off the Queensland coast. Drawing upon his bush carpentry skills, he constructed, with local materials and his own hands, a one-room slab hut and a rudimentary kitchen. He was to reside at this spot, with his long-suffering wife, for the next quarter century. In time, he replaced the hut with a bungalow in the Queensland tropical style, complete with verandahs and surrounding orchard and vegetable plot. Modeling himself on Robinson Crusoe and Henry David Thoreau, he learned to subsist off the land and from the sea, made friends with the local aborigines, scavenged for fragments of civilization cast up on the shore, kept a wary eye out for crocodiles, and eventually produced the classic memoir *The Confessions of a Beachcomber*. Long before the days of off-the-grid technology—solar collectors, wireless communications, composting toilets, desalination equipment, and all the other gear you can now find on survivalist Web sites—he lived contentedly as a sunburned, antipodean Adam in a garden of coral, and crafted some of the finest nature writing of his time.

You can still find *Confessions* in Australian secondhand bookstores, but a stone grave cairn in the jungle is the only remaining trace of Beachcomber's house today.

Meanwhile, shacked up on Hiva Oa with a local thirteen-year-old, Gauguin wasn't penning Presbyterian prayers or meticulously observing the habits of sea turtles. When he wasn't occupied with orgies, drinking, shooting up on morphine, meddling in colonial politics, and spreading syphilis among the local kids, he was feverishly fabricating a mythic Tahiti—a place that never was—for consumption in Paris. Arriving in Papeete a decade earlier, expecting an unspoiled Eden, he had been disappointed to discover a dreary colonial town run by bureaucrats and clerics. He had first removed himself to the more isolated district of Mataiea, where he took up residence in a thatched hut, and began painting his glorious pictures of golden Tahitian women in attitudes and settings cooked up from images of Borobudur reliefs, Parthenon friezes, Egyptian tomb paintings, glowering *tikis* from pre-colonial Polynesia, the romantic travel writings of Pierre Loti, and much else. He had not found paradise, but he had discovered that he could create it from the contents of his well-stocked memory, and nobody in far-off Europe would know the difference.

After a brief and disastrous trip back to Paris, he had returned to Tahiti, made himself a new home at Punaauia, and painted the huge, mesmerizing *Where Do We Come From? What Are We? Where Are We Going?*—the centerpiece of the Boston show. Then in 1901, for what he must have known would be the last act, he sailed to Hiva Oa. Here, at Atuona, he built the House of Pleasure. It was a gabled structure on stilts, with woven coconut walls, coconut thatch roof, a workspace underneath, and a steep flight of steps up to the front door. The interior was decorated with pornographic photographs he had purchased in Egypt—which, as the locals tell it, he liked to show schoolchildren while he groped them. The heavy wooden doorframe was derived from Maori prototypes he had seen in Auckland, and was carved with savagely voluptuous erotica. It was inscribed, "Be mysterious," and "Be in love and you will be happy." He died alone in this house, two years later, among emblems of the cultural displacement he had so desperately struggled to achieve. These were not so different, as we can see now, from the clock, iron bed, washstand, stove, and cooking utensils—products of bourgeois, industrialized Europe—that expressed an equally powerful aspiration to otherness in the house of Mapuhi.

Dear Mister Secretary of Defense:

Nobody—not even Seymour Hersh—ever called bad architecture a war crime. As the political firestorm over the Abu Ghraib torture pictures threatens to consume you, that's worth pondering. Dogs and beatings and electric shocks are simply too crude for your purposes, and those dummies who do the dirty work have digital cameras. It all gets out onto the Internet, and then there's hell to pay. Better to take human operators out of the loop, and just let prison design features help the evildoers to provide actionable intelligence.

It isn't rocket science, and you can probably outsource the necessary design and construction work to civilian contractors. Building codes protect the health and safety of occupants, so, by inverting the principles of codes, you can reverse their effects. Handbooks for interior climate, lighting, and acoustic designers precisely define environmental comfort zones, so take careful note of those and stay well outside of them. Architects usually go for environments that provide legibility, a sense of place, privacy, and basic human dignity, but they don't always succeed, so you can learn a lot from where they go wrong.

The human factors handbooks used by furniture designers provide a good place to start. These describe the requirements for comfortable human posture. Force posture outside of the specified limits, and you immediately get into what the torture trade calls "stress positions." You can simply make cells too small to fully lie down in, and if challenged on this by some bleeding heart, you can claim that the space standards are determined by your thriftiness with the taxpayer's dollar. If that does not suffice, you can make inmates stand or crouch for long periods, with their arms extended, until they are exhausted. As long as there are no observers around, you can up the stress further by balancing hooded inmates on boxes or chairs, and beating or shocking them whenever they teeter and seem ready to fall.

Thermal comfort zones are surprisingly narrow, so desert climates—very hot during the day, and often quite cold at night—offer many creative opportunities. At Guantanomo Bay, you can also take advantage of excessive humidity and the tropical bugs. Budgets are tight, so it's just common sense to construct prisons with as little insulation and sun protection as possible. Where you do happen to have air-conditioning, turn it way up to the shiver point. You can magnify the effects by denying prisoners clothing and blankets. For the really stubborn ones, try locking them up in sealed shipping containers left out in the sun: the temperature will rise very rapidly, and if you pull them out just before they die, you may finally get some cooperation.

Really bad lighting can also be effective. Jailers have long known, of course, that confinement in pitch-black dungeons will quickly adjust prisoner attitudes. But you can now mix it up. Modern electrical systems provide the complementary possibility of holding prisoners, twenty-four hours a day, in brilliantly illuminated, white-walled cells. Add continuous loud noise and prodding at any sign of drowsiness, and you produce sleep deprivation, depression, and psychosis—which definitely helps. It's amazing what the simple absence of a light switch and earplugs can do.

Modern plumbing is an expensive luxury that the taxpayer is not going to want to provide, and the detainees are filthy anyway, so it's best practice to build prisons without fancy sanitation systems. This forces inmates to remain for long periods in close proximity to their own stinking waste. You can use occasional cleanups, and brief access to one of the few showers, as rewards for cooperation. If troublemakers demand increased access to water, just strap them down and hold them under for a while. No need for vermin-proofing, either; rats, scorpions, and sand vipers just add to the coalition of the willing.

Disorientation is always very effective, and featureless environments help. But you can most economically achieve it by keeping prisoners hooded for long periods. This technique was pioneered at Pentonville Prison, in London, in the 1840s. It was intended to help reform prisoners, but it mostly ended up sending them straight to Bedlam. As our psych-ops people have noted, you can expect the same result today. Who knows what they might reveal as they babble? And let's just say, as the

Commander in Chief has put it, that they will no longer be a problem to the United States.

You may have noticed that the architecture of the Muslim world expresses a deep respect for personal privacy, embodies some strong conventions about gender roles, and is generally reticent about displays of naked human flesh. This suggests an opportunity to operate not only at the very basic ergonomic level, but also on a more sophisticated cultural plane. If you strip inmates naked they will, of course, feel vulnerable and humiliated. Better yet, in this context, they will know that the contempt is directed not only at them personally, but also—and even more tellingly—at their culture and religion. Some pointing and grinning helps to reinforce the message. There is plenty of room for creativity with women's underwear, degrading sex acts, and colorful sexual invitations and threats. If the operatives take photographs, they can get still more mileage by showing them—as gleeful trophy pictures—to inmate family and friends. This adds great shame, and often the mere threat of it elicits cooperation from the most recalcitrant subjects. And the beautiful thing is, there isn't a mark on them. Your lawyers should have no difficulty in demonstrating that this doesn't meet the technical definition of "torture."

You need deniability, of course. It's best to avoid giving explicit orders for these measures. It will eventually get out, do-gooding busybodies like the Red Cross and Amnesty will get on your case, and senators will start asking questions. Fortunately though, it isn't necessary. If you set the right tone, by talking endlessly about crusades, clashes of civilizations, and the superiority of our values to theirs, people will know what is expected of them. You can encourage tame talk-show hosts, like Rush Limbaugh, to say things like, "They are the ones who are subhuman." Contractors need the work, so you can count on them to create prisons that express contempt for the inmates and the unconstrained power of the guards to do whatever they like. Remember, we make our buildings, and then our buildings make us. If anyone objects, just tell Fox News that even talking about this stuff aids the enemy.

Above all, be subtle. If you go at it too blatantly, some of our own citizens might begin to resist. They might rebel against the culture of bigotry, dehumanization, and hatred that inevitably produces My Lais and Abu Ghraibs, refuse complicity in immoral and illegal policies, and show the world what democratic values are all about—by throwing the scoundrels out at the next election.

Edmund Burke's famous distinction between the sublime and the beautiful—between big, bad things that filled the mind with delightful horror, and small, smooth objects of love—was *so* eighteenth-century. It summarized just about everything you needed to know about the obsessions of contemporary artists and designers, neatly capturing the contrast between wild beasts and innocent girls, awful chasms and rolling hillsides, vast craggy edifices and delicate details. Today we can learn as much about the preoccupations of our own time from the aesthetic categories of hip-hop, laid down to rhyme patterns and rhythms that would surely have caused Alexander Pope to pop a pentameter.

Hip-hop aesthetic terminology is often defiantly obscure, and detailed exegesis demands some resourceful scholarship, like that once required by the subtleties of "sharawaggi" or "shibui." In any case, it probably shouldn't be attempted by a middle-aged white guy. But a few terms have made it into the linguistic mainstream. "Wack" is a useful addition to the lexicon of critical disapproval, though I would not expect to hear it any time soon from Ada Louise Huxtable in the *Wall Street Journal*. And "bling bling" has recently secured a place in the *Oxford English Dictionary*.

The term first showed up on the late-90s hit album *Chopper City in the Ghetto*, by B.G. and the New Orleans rap family Cash Money Millionaires. The track titled "Bling Bling," with its repetitive, hypnotic chorus, celebrates giving up the street life and flossin' new wealth—flashy platinum and diamonds, custom chromed cars, Rolex watches, and diamond-draped women. After Lil' Turk, Lil' Wayne, Manny Fresh, and Juvenile have taken their turns with the beat, Baby Gangsta comes back to boast: "You have to wear shades just to stand on side of me." Then he signs off with the onomatopoeic couplet:

All day my phone ringin bling bling bling
Can see my earring for a mile bling bling.

These days, anything that flamboyantly flashes and glitters gets classified as bling. Diamond-encrusted watches, bracelets, and chains from Jacob the Jeweler, teeth slugged up with platinum-capped gold from Mr. Bling, Hummers and Escalades with suede seats and chrome dubs, and Snoop Dogg's customized Cadillac Snoop DeVille define the canon. But nice suburban girls (not the sort that Baby would refer to as iced-up hoes) also get bling on their fingers for their engagements. Tasteful table settings get a dash of bling from crystal and silver. And the Roc-A-Fella organization (an enterprise that has more in common with Martha Stewart Living than just a criminal record or two) gives the full aspirational lifestyle marketing treatment to the increasingly mainstream bling of Dash—Damon Dash, Victoria Beckham's hip-hop mogul beau.

In architecture we can now see that, long before Baby was born, Morris Lapidus's exuberant hotel designs made him the Godfather of Bling. The Miami Beach master's unashamed excesses were not much approved of by his mainstream modernist contemporaries. But, at the height of the go-go nineties—the precise cultural moment when *Chopper City* was bursting on the scene—Frank Gehry gave up the street life of chain-link and plywood for which he had become famous, and recast himself as the new king of built bling with the Bilbao Guggenheim. It was like Bob Dylan forsaking acoustic guitar for electric. The exterior cladding of the Guggenheim was titanium—the platinum of sheet metal. The curved forms produced vivid, dynamic highlights. As you approached through the austere and gloomy Bilbao street grid, a blaze of glitter opened up, like a metal-mouth grin, at the end of the road.

Urban planners started to talk about the "Bilbao effect"—the expression of a city's dump-the-drab aspirations, and the attraction of economic activity to support them, by attention-grabbing buildings. A few adventurous architects were ready, like Damon Dash with his Rocawear clothing line, to seize the cultural moment and give it fresh and compelling design expression:

Bling bling
Everytime I come around yo city
Bling bling

Gehry himself led the way. He quickly followed Bilbao with the Experience Music Project—a museum of popular music and a sort of shrine to Jimi Hendrix—in Seattle. Here the rock and roll roots of the design are explicit. The exterior form—as you can clearly see from the nearby Space Needle—is that of a smashed Fender guitar, right down to the broken strings. When you visit on a sunny day, the candy-paint megablobs throb with specularity—flaunting the sorts of optical effects that custom car stylings and ray-traced computer renderings fetishize. The red- and blue-coated metal surfaces pop white-hot highlights, and these move, in complex ways, through the lacy cast shadows of foliage. Meanwhile, reflections in the bronze metallic surfaces surreally shift the colors of the adjacent street, evoking (for aging baby-boomers, anyway) the memory of Hendrix's traffic lights turning blue on Sundays. There are acid-trip, buckled, and distorted reflections of the adjacent roller coasters and monorail tracks. And each surface reflects its neighbors, the reflections of its neighbors, and so on like Grandmaster Flash back spinning. Near the entrance, right on cue, the light bouncing back from a semi-transparent iridescent wall produces a convincing purple haze.

At the recently opened Disney Concert Hall in Los Angeles, as you might expect from the high-culture program, the frozen music isn't so funkdafied. The exterior curved surfaces were originally designed for execution in smoothly milled stone, which would have generated almost neo-classical effects of graduated shading and cast shadow. But construction was long delayed, Gehry and his talented team had learned much from Bilbao and Experience Music in the meantime, and the outside was eventually done in stainless steel. The resulting color effects are less amped-up, but the polished surfaces still zing plenty of bling in the Tinseltown sunshine. There is so much of it, in fact, that you can't touch the stainless on a sunny day, and nearby apartment owners have complained of getting grilled in their living rooms by the bouncing rays.

Finally, at MIT's Stata Center—a huge laboratory building now nearing completion on the Cambridge campus—Gehry has brought his extended exploration of architecture as the masterly, correct, and magnificent play of bling in ray-space to a crackling conclusion. Here, instead of composing a discrete object in the landscape, he has deployed volumes to generate a varied, village-like texture with numerous spiky protrusions, jagged crevices, unexpected transparencies, and ambiguous interplays on interior and exterior space. Chunky metal shapes tumble, like flamboyant costume jewelry, down the décolletage between two brick towers. There are metal curved surfaces to mirror passing clouds, brilliantly colored cubist shapes, and matte surfaces strategically placed to serve as receptors for shading, shadows, reflections, and patches of sunlight. As it happens, I see it from my office window. I watch the facets rapping to the rhythms of the sun, and I can't help recalling the whispered mutter of Hendrix against a tire-squeal of feedback guitar: "Excuse me while I kiss the sky."

Soixante-huitards weep! Forty years on from the Free Speech Movement, the Summer of Love that soon followed, the rowdy streets of '68, and the sweet, gentle, impossible hopes the sixties briefly nurtured—that there'd be swinging, swaying, music playing, and whatever—we find ourselves confronted with a mad Summer of Hatred. Politics, pop culture, and a new theatrics of urban space have conspired once again to construct the cultural moment. This time it's by inverting that sappy old hippy rhetoric of peace and love with a flower in your hair, and substituting a harsh global babble of smugly justified violence, cynically spun media spectacle, force-fed security paranoia, and—around the world, that brand new beat—killing in the street.

Mel Gibson's *The Passion of the Christ*, a splattery snuff pic about the most famous homicide in history, kicked off this bloody season with a box-office bang. The execution and dismemberment videos that the terrorist underground has been churning out with increasing frequency can't match the Passion's production values, but they follow the same formula—

making their point by showing us some symbolically freighted victim gruesomely suffering and dying for our sins. They are low-budget, single-camera indie jobs, with bad lighting and casts of amateurs, but they have effectively appropriated Hollywood's language of screen violence—and they can rely upon grisly authenticity in place of costly special effects.

As the days have grown hotter, the death spectacles have gone on location—to the streets of Baghdad, Jerusalem, Gaza, and whatever other public places happen to appeal to the scenery scouts. There is a simple, inexpensive, and now-familiar recipe. You need an explosive device, and some handy delivery system—a pedestrian, a car, a cellphone wired to a device hidden in a culvert, or a missile. You get maximum bang for your buck if you can hit a symbolically significant target at some crucial moment, but random targeting and timing work too. As soon as there are smoke plumes and charred body parts the camera crews will rush to the scene, and—thanks to modern telecommunications—your made-for-television street theater will be out on the networks within minutes. It's better distribution than you can get from Disney, and you don't have to negotiate with Michael Eisner.

Unless they were dumb enough to haul in a wooden horse full of guys with swords (a weapon of mass destruction that was probably just as mythical as those conjured up by George W. Bush), the ancients didn't have to contend with this sort of thing in the agora. You might get an occasional knifing, but that was about the extent of it. Threats of violence never shut the central civic space down, nor did security arrangements. The agora both symbolized the right of citizens to assemble freely to speak their minds and provided the practical means. Today, by contrast, zones of rigorously controlled access are taking over the hearts of our cities. The anti-agora—a space defended against the theatrics of terror, but consequently no longer available for free assembly and expression either, and devoted instead to ritualized political spectacle for the television cameras—is the next big thing in twenty-first-century civics.

London caught a chilling glimpse of the anti-agora when President Bush visited last November. The presidential motorcade sped through closed streets, carefully segregated from the protestors who thronged Whitehall and Trafalgar Square. For the duration of the visit, grim security cordons organized the city's public space according to the principles of apartheid rather than those of the democratic polis. Even if they had wanted to, the separate-but-unequal sides had no possibility of looking into each other's faces or directly confronting each other's arguments; they occupied themselves, instead, with scripted performances designed to catch the attention of the international media.

For the recent Democratic National Convention in Boston, the Secret Service ordered a state-of-the-art, $50 million anti-agora in the area that city's director of homeland security described as "the seat of liberty." ("You attack that," he said, "it's the very heart of America.") The convention site was the FleetCenter, a featureless, fortress-like sports stadium that squats in a busy corner of downtown, not far from icons of the Revolutionary era like Faneuil Hall, the Old State House, and the Freedom Trail. Not only were the approaches cordoned off, nearby North Station was shut down as well, as were nearly forty miles of surrounding major roadways. The Central Artery—the city's main commuter thoroughfare—was closed from Braintree to Woburn. Downtown workers were advised to stay at home for the duration and watch it all on television. But, if you were somehow able to make it into the area, past the bag searches and bomb-sniffing dogs, and you had the necessary hard-to-get permits, you could demonstrate in the Free Speech Zone—a nearby patch of dirt that was grudgingly set aside for the purpose after some troublemakers went to court and demanded the right to be present within sight and sound of the delegates. What about speech *outside* the zone? You didn't need George Orwell's ear for doublespeak to get the message.

There is much more of this to come, as the Summer of Hatred creeps on. When the Republican National Convention comes to Madison Square Garden in New York in September, the city will face a lockdown enforced by interlocking steel barricades, mounted police, and pepper spray. Protest permits are being refused for sites throughout Manhattan, even Central Park; the mayor says that crowds would be bad for the grass, and has suggested Queens instead. When crowds do manage to assemble, they will find themselves confined within pens formed by swiftly deployed barricades and lines of riot-equipped police closing off both ends of city blocks. Meanwhile, in London, *The Observer* has reported that "intelligence chiefs" want to set up a "sterile security zone" around Westminster and the Houses of Parliament, from Trafalgar Square to Millbank.

The anti-agora serves the common interests of hard, violent men at the political extremes, who use each other's outrages to justify their actions, but whose real targets are the messy, challenging, sometimes disturbing forms of expression that characterize genuinely open and democratic society— free thought, free speech, free movement, and free assembly. When the centers of our cities are closed and secured against their own citizens, we can have no doubt that the hard men are winning.

I once met Ray Bradbury, and he told me of writing his early stories on coin-in-the-slot typewriters in the basement of the UCLA library. Pounding the keyboard against the clock, the author of *Fahrenheit 451* must have developed a keen sense of the human care and effort represented by a page of text, and thus the pathos of its destruction. I recalled this as I watched Michael Moore's carefully understated treatment, in *Fahrenheit 9/11*, of the violent annihilation of the World Trade Center towers. Moore played the sounds of the fatal moments over a black screen, then simply cut to a blizzard of paper floating down onto the streets of Manhattan—thousands upon thousands of sheets suddenly ripped from the desks and files where they had been so carefully cradled, and hurled high into the morning air. You think immediately of the hands that held them.

Moore needed an unexpected metaphor because the established filmic language of urban destruction had for too long been associated with cornball science fiction and disaster films. Resorting to it in this context would have cheapened a genuine tragedy. If he had directly shown the fiery airplane impacts on the big screen, they would have seemed like special effects from an Irwin Allen movie.

The lineage of urban mayhem and havoc films extends back to the 1930s at least. The MGM musical melodrama *San Francisco* is my nomination for the civic destruction ur-flick. It has everything: direction by the estimable W. S. Van Dyke, Clark Gable as the handsome, heel-without-a-heart saloon owner Blackie Norton, Jeanette MacDonald as the sweet chanteuse to whom he loses the organ he didn't know he had, and knockout special effects of the 1906 earthquake. It was the golden age of the star-vehicle studio epic, and this is one of the masterpieces of the genre. You see a beautifully crafted recreation of the Barbary Coast, and then you see it convincingly crumble and burn. The memory of the Big One must still have been fresh and terrifying for members of the effects team, and it shows. They make you believe. Then the closing scene, to the eponymous title tune, shows a rebuilt city of shiny skyscrapers by the Bay.

Both in sci-fi disaster movies and in arch-sci laboratories, the postwar decades were the heyday of the model-maker's craft. While the boffins were busy measuring daylighting under artificial skies, shooting beams of light through smoke-filled acoustic models of auditoriums, cranking up the wind tunnels, and carefully attaching strain gauges to scaled-down structural frames, the special effects artists were creating architectural and urban miniatures that would disintegrate convincingly for the cameras. There must have been some crossover of scientific knowledge; in both cases, if you want verisimilitude, you must understand failure modes and scaling effects—such as the differences between ocean waves and water slopping around in tanks.

The fifties model-smasher that everyone remembers is *Godzilla*. In its beautiful new reconstruction, it holds up remarkably well as a dark allegory on the dangers of the nuclear age. But its effects look laughable today—just a guy in a lizard suit stomping some generic chunks of Tokyo. The high-camp high point came when Ray Bradbury and the great stop-action animator Ray Harryhausen teamed up on *It Came from 20,000 Fathoms*, in which another supersized saurian splashes around the Manhattan docks, walks through brick walls, crunches a few cars underfoot, munches a cop like a canapé, and smacks down the Coney Island rollercoaster.

In 1974, the shake and bake twins—*Earthquake* and *The Towering Inferno*—started a cycle of big-budget effects operas in which urban destruction spectacles aren't just background, but provide the narrative climaxes themselves. *The Towering Inferno* was a sequel without a predecessor—clearly presenting itself as *Tower of Babel II*, and similar dramas of technological hubris followed by cataclysmic come-uppance have hit the screen at regular intervals since. The trick, in recycling the theme, has been to substitute some new type of very large constructed object—an airliner, an ocean liner, maybe a French airport. *Earthquake* established the formula consisting of (1) high-concept title, (2) iconic city taking a terrible beating, (3) some uncontrollable phenomenon doing the dirty work, and (4) lots of people dead but the principal protagonists pluckily surviving, to swelling music, to start cleaning up the mess. It has been followed by *Armageddon, Avalanche, Deep Impact, Godzilla* (a lousy 1998 remake), *Independence Day, Meteor, Swarm, Tidal Wave, Tornado,* and *Volcano.* Watch out for *Locusts, Smog, Gridlock,* and *Redevelopment.*

Since the seventies, digital animation has increasingly superseded scale models and stop motion in Hollywood's most advanced effects shops. Simultaneously, the old, model-based architectural science laboratories have faded away, to be replaced be three-dimensional geometric modeling software combined with engineering analysis, simulation, and perspective rendering techniques. Now, if you want to see what would happen to a building subjected to impact, crushing, shaking, wind, fire, smoke, explosion, water, or death rays, you first digitally model its geometry and relevant physical properties, then do some applied physics computations, and finally produce photorealistic animations of the outcomes. At successive SIGGRAPH computer graphics conferences over the years, more and more amazing digital techniques have been announced—to be taken up first by Hollywood and the military (who have the money to spend on the latest and costliest), and then eventually to trickle down into architectural practice.

This summer's up-to-the-minute effects showcase is Roland Emmerich's *The Day After Tomorrow,* which solemnly undertakes to demonstrate that global warming is a bad thing. The plot is risible and the performances from some talented actors rarely rise above career limiting, but the numerous simulated destruction sequences by Digital Domain are fabulously over-the-top Oscar bait. Los Angeles is flattened by tornados, Tokyo is hit by giant hailstones, and New York is engulfed by a wall of water that froths at the steps of the Public Library and sends a freighter floating up Fifth Avenue. Most of the Northern Hemisphere eventually gets frozen solid, leaving a thickly frosted Statue of Liberty staring out across a new Arctic landscape (recalling *Planet of the Apes*), and warmth-seeking refugees fleeing south across the Mexican border.

Ironically though, the most memorable of all these cities in extremis epics—Stanley Kramer's *On the Beach*, set in 1950s Melbourne—does not rely upon special effects at all. To suggest a world turned uninhabitable by clouds of nuclear radiation, it simply shows us empty city streets. As the deadly clouds drift south, and the last people left on earth sing Waltzing Matilda into the night, you see that the silencing of a city's voices, not the destruction of its concrete and steel, is the ultimate tragedy. Bourke Street and Collins Street were still out there, but they no longer meant a thing.

It never feels quite right to walk around Los Angeles. It's not just that the streets aren't pedestrian friendly; it's also that you can't get to know the city that way. The scale is too large, you're moving too slowly, and you're far too close to the dusty ground. You need a car—preferably air-conditioned, with a good sound system. Then you can sweep west from the towers of downtown onto the elevated concrete ribbon of the Santa Monica Freeway, feel the vastness of the mountain-fringed Los Angeles Basin as you head for the ocean, and swing north along the Pacific Coast Highway for the wide beaches of Malibu. You can wind along Sunset Boulevard or Mulholland Drive, then cross Sepulveda Pass into the hot San Fernando Valley. You can cruise the endless boulevards with the kids at night, climb the mysterious canyons into the Hollywood Hills, and inch along with the rush-hour commuters on the 405. There are moments when you crest a rise to see the Hollywood sign shimmering in the smoggy distance, or round a bend to confront miles of coastline stretching away to the horizon.

Like a well-edited movie, though, L.A. is composed not only of wide shots that establish the context, but also of close-ups. The cuts come at the points where you park your car to enter more intimate settings, and the scenes always end when you jump back in to drive off. Many of these enclaves are oases of privacy and privilege—the leafy yards of suburban homes with their Hockney-blue pools, gated residential communities, the green, bungalow-filled grounds of the Bel Air Hotel. Some, like the gas stations and strip malls portrayed by Ed Ruscha, are just momentary asides from the automobile world. Yet others— the innumerable shopping malls and cineplexes, office towers, Disneyland, the Disney Concert Hall, even Rafael Moneo's L.A. Cathedral—form an archipelago of tiny city-states with parking lots (adjacent or beneath, depending on the urban density) instead of ports. It works best when there's valet.

The most memorable fictional portraits of L.A. transmute this spatial structure directly into plot. Raymond Chandler's world-weary detectives encounter their villains and seductresses after driving to emblematic settings in Pasadena, Chinatown, and Bunker Hill and finding places to park. Walter Mosley's Easy Rawlins—postmodern and black—spends more of his time in South-Central, Watts, and the tawdry back streets of the San Gabriel Valley, but the pattern is self-consciously the same. If you watch old episodes of *Dragnet* with a structuralist's eye, you will see how the urgent missions of LAPD cruisers generate archetypal retribution narratives from urban geography. It's the same with *CHiPs*—but on motorcycles. And in the pivotal scene of *Sunset Boulevard* Gloria Swanson drives to Paramount, with her sad and knowing old chauffeur at the wheel, to see Cecil B. De Mille.

In Paris, by contrast, it doesn't feel right to drive—though, of course, the Parisians now do so in droves on their proliferating motorways. Things go by too fast. You want to linger and see more, but you can't. This was, after all, the city of Baudelaire and the *flâneur*—the leisured stroller among the crowds, who inspected the curiosities of the emerging modern metropolis with a cool and ironic eye. Unlike shoppers, commuters, and tourists with guidebooks, the *flâneur* did not have a definite goal: he was driven by whim and momentary curiosity, and he was always open to diversion. The inner life of a changing city was revealed to him—so he hoped, at least—through chance encounters and unexpected details.

Baudelaire's Paris was a city of narrow streets, labyrinthine alleys, squares, parks, cafés, windows, thresholds, and tantalizing glimpses. The sidewalks could become stages for dandies, but the anonymous throng could always provide cover. For the artist, as Baudelaire famously proclaimed in "The Painter of Modern Life," it was a place to immerse oneself, to gather fragmentary impressions from the surrounding multiplicity and flux, and eventually to transform these into images or texts. After Haussmann, Mitterrand, and the traffic engineers, it isn't quite the same, and after a pretty good working over by Marxist and feminist cultural theorists, the idea of innocent *flânerie* isn't either. But for all that, Paris remains a place that gradually gives up its secrets to the curious and patient wanderer.

To the figures of the *flâneur* and the driver as knowers of the city through their characteristic modes of engagement, we can now add that of the skateboarder—or, in a fashionable European variant, the *traceur* engaged in *parkour*. In contrast to the solitary *flâneur*, skateboarders mostly roam in small tribes, spurn crowds, and gravitate to the neglected and deserted urban margins where they will not be bothered by unsympathetic cops and security guards. The Californian kids who pioneered skateboard culture favored empty swimming pools in deserted backyards, disused parking lots and loading docks, and after-hours schoolyards for perfecting their gravity-defying, quasi-suicidal maneuvers—together with some piss-off-the-oldies forays into hilly city streets. These days, you can find skateboarders putting clattering wheels to pavement in otherwise spooky and silent office plazas at the weekend, boarded-up shopping centers, and the loneliest of failed public spaces. Insouciant celebrants of the desolate, they are closer in spirit to J. G. Ballard's anomic witnesses of gathering urban distress than to Baudelaire's rather smug stroller-gazers in the glittering capital of the nineteenth century.

The practice of *parkour* (circuit), which seems to have originated in Lisse, France in the late eighties, is less self-consciously disaffected and less wedded to gritty marginality, but equally obsessed with speed and risk. It is a youthfully exuberant way to slip the surly bonds of the paved ground plane and valorize the vertical. The goal of a *traceur* is to run, jump, vault, twist, and climb through an urban environment in as fast and fluid a way as possible. Architectural obstacles are taken as adversaries to grapple with—even to the extent of heart-stopping handrail surfing and building-to-building leaping—rather than as inert lumps of stuff to be circled around, peered at, or parked beside. Flowing transitions between moves are as important as the moves themselves. The roots of all this are clearly to be found not only in skateboarding and surfing, but also in martial arts, break dancing, and video games.

Just as Baudelaire personified the *flâneur* as a self-effacing painter slipping in and out of the Parisian crowds, then returning to his studio to jot down sketches, so the *Spiderman* movies have provided the apotheosis of the *traceur*. Spiderman is a kid from the suburbs, but he loves the close-packed towers of Manhattan and the vertiginous perches they provide. Underneath his spiffy spandex and mask, he is just a shy and insecure teenager who, appealingly, yearns for the usual teenage things. But he can also become—like the dandy Baudelaire putting on his pink gloves to strut the boulevards—a confident urban performance artist who inhabits the city in a new way, and lets the rest of us imagine that we might do so too.

Recently, while extracting some money from a Zurich cash machine, I caught an unexpected glimpse of Le Corbusier. His portrait—complete with black-rimmed spectacles shoved up onto the forehead and I'm-Corb-you're-not look—confronted me from a Swiss ten-franc note. It turns out that he is just one member of an extensive lineup, on colorful notes of various denominations, of certified Swiss cultural heroes: Arthur Honegger, Sophie Taeuber-Arp, Alberto Giacometti, Charles Ferdinand Ramuz, and Jacob Burckhardt. Perhaps it is the Swiss National Bank's long-delayed response to Harry Lime's wicked observation in *The Third Man*: "In Italy, for thirty years under the Borgias, they had warfare, terror, murder, bloodshed, but they produced Michelangelo, Leonardo da Vinci, and the Renaissance. In Switzerland they had brotherly love, they had five hundred years of democracy and peace, and what did that produce? The cuckoo clock."

Historically, banknotes have mostly served as visual projections of the power of the state—the body solely authorized to print money, and you'd better not forget it! They have carried images of sovereigns, presidents, generals, liberators, fathers-of-countries, treasuries, palaces, and that sort of thing. American greenbacks continue stolidly in this vein, with portraits of presidents on the front, Washington monuments on the back, and the inscription "In God we trust." The dollar bill has the Great Seal of the United States, with an eagle, lots of Latin, and that weird pyramid with the Eye of God radiating some sort of electromagnetic energy from the apex. But one architect does make it. Thomas Jefferson (of course, he was a president too, in the days when it did not seem absurd to imagine cultured intellectuals in that role) first appeared on the 1928 two-dollar bill. One of his great projects, Monticello, was shown on the back. He is still there on the current two, but Monticello has been replaced by an engraving of John Trumbull's "The Signing of the Declaration of Independence." The two is famously rare, but Jefferson also appears, with a relief of Monticello, on the ubiquitous, though nearly useless, nickel coin.

More recently, as the current Swiss series illustrates, banknotes have often played a less overtly political role, and have functioned instead as expressions of local cultural pride within a globalizing world. The Australians began it, in the 1960s, when they dumped pounds, shillings, and pence in favor of a new decimal currency system. In a fit of colonial nostalgia, the government of the day initially suggested that the new currency unit should be named the royal, but this proposal was greeted with raucous derision, and the bright new bills ended up being Australian dollars. The 1966 ten-dollar note carried a picture of the convict architect Francis Greenway on the obverse, and the bard of the bush Henry Lawson on the reverse. Greenway, who was a talented exponent of colonial Georgian adapted to Australian conditions, designed many of Sydney's earliest buildings, including the Government House and Supreme Court. He had been transported for forgery in 1814—an ironic detail that occasioned much Sydneyside smirking when the Greenway ten first appeared—and he was eventually dismissed as government architect in a dispute over fees.

In the decades since, as an hour with Google will confirm, architects and their works have frequently shown up in the national dream-teams portrayed on currency. Not surprisingly, Christopher Wren quickly got the nod from the Bank of England selectors, and appeared on the 1981 fifty-pound note, together with a plan of Saint Paul's. It was a large note that did not find its way into many wallets, but it is pleasant to imagine that it gave a whiff of architectural culture to used car and drug deals. In 1999, to celebrate Glasgow's designation as UK City of Architecture and Design, Clydesdale Bank responded with a portrait of Alexander "Greek" Thomson on a twenty-pound note, with Thomson's Holmwood House and Charles Rennie Mackintosh's "Lighthouse" building on the back.

Mostly, of course, you find the usual suspects. Mimar Sinan, with the Selimiye Mosque, is on Turkish ten-thousand-lira notes from the 1980s. Jože Plečnik, in a very stylish shaker hat, appeared on the first five-hundred-tolar note when Slovenia introduced its own currency in 1991. Victor Horta showed up on a Belgian two-thousand-franc note, in the company of James Ensor on the hundred, Adolphe Sax (inventor of the saxophone) on the two-hundred, René Magritte (sadly, unaccompanied by the "this is not a banknote" inscription you might expect) on the five-hundred, and the expressionist Constant Permeke on the thousand. And Antoni Gaudi's image, naturally, is on coins from Catalunya.

Some more obscure currencies remind you that the canon implied by today's international architectural discourse has some very arbitrary limits. Portraits of the great medieval polymath al-Farabi appear on tenge notes from Kazakhstan in the 1990s, together with drawings that recall his important contributions to (among many other things) architectural theory. The Armenian architect Alexander Tamanyan is famous enough in his home country to be portrayed on the 1999 five-hundred-dram note, with the main square of Yerevan on the back, but a Google search on his name produces few hits. Nikola Fichev, the most prominent Bulgarian architect of the nineteenth century, has his face on the 1997 Bulgarian two-thousand-leva note, along with a selection of his works in the National Revival style. As far as the schools and magazines are concerned, these might as well be imaginary characters from *Da Ali G Show*.

The current Euro banknotes continue this tradition of architectural imagery, but to opposite effect—serving to obscure rather than to celebrate local cultural identity. They resulted from an elaborate competition process run in 1996 by the Council of the European Monetary Institute, and eventually won by Robert Kalina, a banknote designer at the Oesterreichische Nationalbank. There are precisely rendered windows and gateways on the fronts of the notes, and bridges on the backs. According to the FAQ website that explains the designs, and seems to have been written by Borges after extensive perusal of Banister Fletcher, "They depict the architectural styles of seven periods in Europe's cultural history: classical for the five-Euro, Romanesque for the ten-Euro, Gothic for the twenty-Euro, Renaissance for the fifty-Euro, baroque and rococo for the hundred-Euro, nineteenth century iron and glass architecture for the two-hundred-Euro, and modern twentieth century architecture for the five-hundred-Euro . . . The images are modeled on the typical architectural style of each period, rather than on specific structures." You look at them uneasily, trying to identify their subjects, until you realize the trick that has been played. They have reduced architecture to generic visual mush, the graphic equivalent of elevator music.

This farrago of Brussels think brings us near to the end of an era that began when emperors started to stamp their likenesses on coins, entered a new phase when the printer and American Founding Father Benjamin Franklin (who, fittingly, appears on the U.S. hundred-dollar bill) published *A Modest Enquiry into the Nature and Necessity of a Paper Currency* in 1729, and has continued into a time of polypropylene banknotes with animated holograms. With credit and debit cards, money transfer networks, and electronic cash, money is now dematerializing and shifting into cyberspace. The electromagnetically encoded bits that flash through networks to credit and debit accounts are invisible tokens in a global system, and they no longer serve the traditional secondary function of carrying and circulating culturally significant images and creating a sense of place. The growing abstraction of money into digital information is stealthily eliminating an ancient, potent means of expressing cultural identity and sustaining local pride.

It's as if Dr. Evil made Mini Us, and it prompts some theological speculation of the sort that wouldn't go down well in Bush-voting, axis of evangelicals territory. If man is created in the image of God, does the recent discovery of Flores man—a meter-high, distinct species of humans that apparently lived on the island until 18,000 years ago—mean that God is shorter than we thought? Or is he homo sapiens-sized after all, just as the artists have always depicted him? But this would mean that those prehistoric Munchkins were all alone in their jungle home, without a size-appropriate God of their own, which does seem discriminatory—at least to us unregenerate Massachusetts liberals. Those unorthodox enough to flirt with postmonotheism might resolve the issue by postulating a separated-at-birth duo, like Arnold Schwarzenegger and Danny DeVito in *Twins*.

Did the Adam and Eve of Flores have their own mini-Garden of Eden (a bit like a miniature golf course, I suppose) with a bonsai-sized apple tree and shrunken serpent? I'm getting out of my depth here, and should perhaps leave that as a seminar topic for Bob Jones and Oral Roberts Universities. Back at my East Coast sink of secular permissiveness, though, we have been distracting ourselves from the thought of four more years of dangerous stupidity by wondering what the buildings and towns of homo floresiensis would have been like if there had been a chance for them to develop. The Flores version of Adam's house in Paradise would, we presume, have been about the size of a large doghouse. The Flores variant of Vitruvian man would have been drawn within a tinier circle. And, of course, the Flores Modulor would have been constructed on a significantly smaller base dimension.

Imagining this architecture is not just a matter of shrinking everything, however. As Galileo pointed out in his pioneering treatise on statics and strength of materials, structural members do not scale linearly; the bones of a mouse have slenderer proportions than the bones of an elephant, and similarly, the buildings of Flores would not only have been smaller but also lighter and probably more graceful than our own. To accommodate the same populations and activities, they would generally have had greater surface-to-volume ratios, which would have reduced thermal efficiency and pushed a greater proportion of construction cost into surface materials. And, since inverse square laws control the propagation of light, radiant heat, and sound, the designs of windows, theaters, and environmental systems would have worked out rather differently at Flores scale.

Bricks would, I suppose, have been scaled to the hands of Flores bricklayers. Perhaps the little fingers of Flores craftsmen would, in general, have enabled extraordinarily fine workmanship, but it seems more likely that the sizes of most joints and details would be about the same as those in our own buildings, since these are largely determined by the properties of materials, the capabilities of manufacturing processes, and the tolerances that are realistically achievable. So the density of detail on architectural surfaces would probably have been different, with (to us) disconcerting effect—much as when we zoom too far in or out on CAD models, or when texture-mapped computer renderings get the scales of surface patterns out of whack.

Designing Flores buildings in your head is not just an amusing thought experiment; it also serves as a vivid reminder that the traditions and practices of architecture are located within a very narrow band in the range from nanoscale structures to galaxies, and that they would be very different if this band expanded, contracted, or shifted. If you watch the famous Eames film *Powers of Ten*, which zooms continuously between the scale extremities of the universe, the scale band at which homo sapiens makes and experiences architecture flashes past in an instant. The scale band at which homo floresiensis would have done so is only slightly displaced from this, but sufficiently enough to work by different rules, and to have different visual and spatial qualities.

Alexander Pope would, no doubt, have been discomfited by the proposition that homo sapiens and homo floresiensis represent different branches in an evolutionary tree (one that possibly contains many more, yet to be discovered), not links in a vast chain of being ordered from end to end by God. But he would have resonated with the thought that there is a close match between the capabilities of our bodies and the possibilities of experience and knowledge offered by our surroundings.

"Why has not man a microscopic eye?" he asked in *Essay on Man*, and briskly responded, "For this plain reason, man is not a fly." If we were built to see smaller things, we would miss out on the experience of larger ones: "Say what the use, were finer optics given, to inspect a mite, not comprehend the heaven?" If our sense of touch were too acute, we would "smart and agonize at every pore." If we were more sensitive to smells, we might "die of a rose in aromatic pain." If we always heard at boom-box volume, so that nature thundered in our ears, we would wish that Heaven had left us still, "the whisp'ring zephyr and the purling rill." It's all for the best. "Who finds not Providence all good and wise, alike in what it gives and what denies?"

Pope's couplets suggest that maintaining the human scale of our surroundings is not only a matter of relating spatial dimensions and proportions to those of the body, but also of fitting visual properties to the intensity and spectral ranges and acuity of the eye, acoustic properties to the capabilities of the ear, aromas to the nose, tastes to the palette, textures to the fingertip, and information flows generally to our cognitive capacities. Very fine print that is difficult to read, highly amplified music that hurts our ears, the overpowering taste of chili peppers, and floods of information from computer screens are all out of scale without sensory apparatus and out of proportion with other experiences. Would these aspects of scale and proportion have affected Flores man exactly as they do to us? There is no way to know for sure, but probably not. They do work out differently for flies, dogs, moles, and bats, for the hearing- and sight-impaired, and for humans equipped with prosthetic devices such as night vision goggles.

The crumbling bones of Flores man teach us that the relationships of architecture to human anatomy and intelligence are more complex and contingent that they had seemed. It will be a lesson worth remembering as technology increasingly supplements evolution, as the boundaries between the human and the artificial are erased, and as new information and medical technologies extend and renew the capabilities of our bodies and minds in increasingly dramatic ways. Now that's what *I* call being born again.

Details? Yoshio Taniguchi doesn't want you to be conscious of them, and he works hard at making them disappear. In the same spirit of scrupulous neo-minimalism, I suppose I should stop right here, and simply present this sentence—tastefully set off with lots of white space—as an artful apercu on New York's new MoMA. Or I could do it as an homage to Jenny Holzer, and scroll it in LED. But they pay me for a thousand words, and too much self-referentiality can be self-defeating (if I say so myself) so it's worth decompressing the headline—running a mental Stuffit to disclose the precise reasons for Taniguchi's success.

The usual problem with architectural minimalism, as anyone who has ever tried it knows, is that buildings are large things made out of many small pieces. You can design a big, simple shape—a rectangular brick panel, say—but particularly from up close, the intricate, small-scale pattern of elements and joints will probably dominate the simplicity of the larger unit. One way to get back to simplicity is to make the individual construction elements as large as possible, so that the discontinuities in the surface are too sparsely distributed to be noticeable.

Another way is to conceal the joints by reducing their sizes and matching their colors and textures to those of the adjacent elements. And yet another way is to reduce the scale of the elements below some visual threshold, so that the surface reads as a uniform texture rather than as a composition of discrete objects. At MoMA, as you might expect, all of these strategies have been deployed with exquisite care and skill—most tellingly, perhaps, on the flawless black curtain wall that fronts 54th Street.

If you have a digital camera, you can actually measure the difference between MoMA's simple surfaces and more complex ones, such as those of Cesar Pelli's polychrome apartment tower next door. A photograph of a simple surface yields a relatively small JPG file, since the JPG compression algorithm takes advantage of the fact that many pixels are the same as their neighbors. But a photograph of a complex surface produces a larger file, since pixels mostly differ from their neighbors. To put the point in slightly different technical terms, there is not much visual signal coming at you from the simple surface, but more being emitted from the complex surface.

A second problem for would-be minimalists—particularly with large programmatically and technically complex buildings—is to control the proliferation of shapes, materials, and spatial relationships that response to practical requirements tends to generate. In contrast to most of the other entrants in the competition he won to get the project, Taniguchi chose to approach his task within the framework of a strict, sober, geometric discipline. The formal language he has deployed is one of rectangular planes and openings that often seem to float in space, arrangements of parallels and perpendiculars, long straight lines, and details everywhere reduced to simple slots— a combination of features that, as sophisticated museum-goers will recognize, was introduced into the gene pool of Modernism by the Barcelona Pavilion. With discreet virtuosity, he demonstrates that nothing more is needed to vary the scales and proportions of spaces as required, convincingly organize the circulation, seamlessly connect to the existing structures, and gracefully nestle into the urban context.

If you were to build a carefully constructed CAD model of the design, you could also measure this parsimony of means. You could quickly create the model by first establishing a very simple vocabulary of rectangular solids and voids, then building up the complete composition by scaling, translating, rotating by ninety degrees, and copying. You would need far fewer commands than if you had to describe it point-by-point and line-by-line, as in a composition of more arbitrarily varied shapes and relationships, such as Frank Gehry's Bilbao Guggenheim. In the argot of CAD-jockeys, you could say that there's a short undo trail for the input process; the tight geometric discipline allows radical compression of the geometric description. There is not a lot of signal coming at you from the geometry, either.

None of this comes cheap. Taniguchi has been widely reported as telling the trustees, "Raise a lot of money for me, I'll give you good architecture. Raise even more money, I'll make the architecture disappear." (Less will cost you more.) But it does the job. The resulting galleries are like iPods—sleek, up-market machines for experiencing art, white boxes that conceal a lot beneath the surface and focus all your attention on what's displayed within a rectangular frame and what's coming in through your earpiece.

The iPod aesthetic is entirely consistent with a position that the Modern has upheld from its inception: art is signal, context is noise, and the task of a museum is to maximize the signal-to-noise ratio. Maybe, post-Duchamp, it implicitly provides art's very definition; art is the stuff that you *present* as signal—that you surround with white space. Don't look here for the relationship of an altarpiece to its church, a Veronese to its palace, or graffiti to its urban setting. Don't expect to see anything of the contexts of use of the objects in the famous Design Collection; here they encounter each other, amid the white, as if upon a dissecting table. With what seems like some gentle self-mockery (Does the Modern actually have a sense of humor?) the visitors themselves become art as you see them from a distance, framed by crisp apertures in the impeccable walls.

You don't get context, but you do get concentration. Seen from across a vast space, Monet's water lilies present themselves as a view through a Corbusian strip window, directly into the garden at Giverny (though they reminded one cranky critic of a soiled band-aid). Confronting you as you turn a corner, Picasso's demoiselles are in your face like rappers. And the enigmatic scribbles of Cy Twombly have never looked so good.

I have often wondered what James Joyce would have made of television. Certainly he was fascinated by the movies. Radio, too; he went on at length, in *Finnegan's Wake*, about a "tolv-tubular daildialler, as modern as tomorrow afternoon and in appearance up to the minute, . . . with a vitaltone speaker." (You should see how Word's spelling and grammar checker just reacted to *that*! Then again, there's a considerable scholarly industry devoted to disentangling Joyce typos—or affirming, as the case may be, that they are *not* typos.) But he didn't get to see the emergence of the television drama series, and that's a pity, because *Ulysses* is clearly the progenitor of shows like *Desperate Housewives*.

Joyce wastes no time in introducing his stars—"stately, plump Buck Mulligan," the intellectual Stephen Dedalus, Leopold Bloom in search of a kidney for breakfast, and Molly Bloom turning over sleepily in her bed. Then he brings them together repeatedly, in various combinations, in episodes set at iconic locations scattered throughout Dublin. (Now they are all on the Joyce tour.) This gives him plenty of space to explore their evolving relationships, and to provide a compelling portrait of the turn-of-the-century Irish capital. It maps onto the *Odyssey*, of course, and it would also map onto a season of weekly television shows. You can imagine the author in Hollywood instead of Trieste, pitching the concept of *Desperate Hibernians* to a producer.

Early sitcoms established the basic formula of the television drama series. As with drawing-room dramas on stage, there was a box set—the living room of stately, plump Jackie Gleason, Tony Hancock, or Desi and Lucy—and it remained constant from episode to episode. Typically there was a studio audience, and there could be one, two, or three cameras, fixed or mobile—depending upon budget and the director's conception of the television tube either as a tiny proscenium arch or as a miniature movie screen. Each episode was a complete narrative, with beginning, middle, and end, plus (the BBC aside) intermissions for commercials, but the entire series could also have plot and character development on a more extended scale.

As production techniques and budgets improved, television drama shed the conventions of the stage, and its dramatic themes moved beyond the domestic. There were comedies and soap operas set in hospitals, jails, offices, schools, department stores, urban hotels, rural inns, airports, casinos, funeral homes, taxi garages, restaurants, bars, Whitehall, and the White House. "Reality" versions dispensed with sets, writers, and professional actors, and relied upon found characters and settings. If there is something left out of this list, it is probably the subject of a pilot in development right now. Future historians will look to the archives of these shows for insight into twentieth-century architectural typology—the equivalent of plowing through Pevsner's *History of Building Types*, but much more entertaining.

With that insouciant disregard for genre boundaries that seems to characterize our era, there has been crossover not only from actual architecture to series settings, but also in the other direction. The *Cheers* bar in Boston, for example, models itself on its television twin, and it has been extensively franchised. Nobody knows your name in the *real* Cheers bar, though; you're a tourist.

Another variant to make an early appearance was the road series, in which each episode has a new setting. This transposes to a new medium the perennial form of the pilgrimage narrative—Homer, Chaucer, Kipling's *Kim*, Kerouac's *On the Road*, and all that silly stuff about hobbits. It has a close parallel in road movies, from *Easy Rider* to *Thelma and Louise* and the recent, wonderful *Motorcycle Diaries*. It provides the opportunity not only to explore plot twists and character development and interaction, but also to build up a film portrait of some extensive and picturesque terrain. The protagonists can be fugitives, pursuers, or searchers after wisdom, experience, and maybe a lost home. They can get their kicks on Route 66, or they can get back to where they once belonged.

For a combination of continuity and variety, the setting of a series can be a particular town or city, providing precisely the sort of opportunity for detailed urban characterization and commentary that Joyce had been after. The ur-production in this genre, I suppose, was *The Prisoner*—that supremely strange sixties show starring Patrick McGoohan and a large white ball with a smoothed, expressionless surface that anticipated the botox look. The seventeen-part series was set—as everyone knew, though it was never explicitly identified—in Clough Williams-Ellis's Welsh seaside fantasy village of Portmeirion. It provided the handsomest portrait ever made of that curious place, and introduced it to millions who would never think of actually visiting. Then came *Dallas*—with its brilliantly engineered representation of a truly mundane and boring city as a redneck Xanadu, and its artful reworking of Jane Austen's contrasts of city and country house manners.

The urban settings currently commanding viewer attention seem to be the Manhattan of *Sex and the City* (now departed from prime time in the U.S., but still wildly popular in syndication); the New Jersey of *The Sopranos*, with its haunting opening sequence of turnpike exits, dreariness, and dead-pan cool; Bikini Bottom, with the pineapple under the sea that houses *Spongebob Squarepants*; and the suburban cul-de-sac of Wisteria Lane that contains the homes of the *Desperate Housewives*. Together they add up to a museum without walls of American material culture in the era of Red State hegemony, from SoHo fashion to Pottery Barn, and from Martha Stewart to the décor of the Club Bada Bing.

The production designer of *Desperate Housewives* was Thomas A. Walsh. When scouting locations, reports the *Los Angeles Times*, he "first turned to those 'Spielberg-like communities'—Stevenson Ranch and Simi Valley—but they were all 'a little too real or a little too beige.'" He eventually settled upon Colonial Street at Universal Studios, a collection of suburban houses left over from earlier films and television series, relocated there in the 1980s. He and his set decorator repainted them in Whisper Violet by Benjamin Moore, built interior rooms for scenes of spying out the windows, fitted them out with whitewashed wood and butcher block, and furnished them from various catalogues as appropriate to the particular characters. The super-sexualized bodies that speak the lines as perfectly as Pixar animations—the Latin hot tomato, the camp-slut California blonde, the underwear-ad muscled male—complete this mise-en-scène, and provide pretty wall decoration themselves when you replay them from your TiVo on a big screen with the sound turned off.

I know the New Urbanists and Prince Charles prefer traditional streets and village greens to cul-de-sacs, but they might want to take a careful look at this. There seems to be a lively sense of community, with plenty of social interaction among the neighbors. And it simply *has* to be more fun than Celebration.

It took just twenty years for the personal computer to go from glamorous, newly invented avatar of the future to drab commodity that anonymous corporations produce and distribute by the millions at the lowest possible price points. IBM's recent sale of its personal computer division to a Chinese outfit that most Americans and Europeans had never heard of is a sure sign that the digital revolution of the late twentieth century is over. Media mania is no more. But as the tumult and the shouting of the journalists and the flacks dies, the captains and the kings of industry depart the hallowed ground of Silicon Valley (retiring to their McMansions to dream of breaking into bio or nano), the legendary labs close their doors one by one, and the Internet bubble of the waning millennium fades into history like tulip frenzy and the great gold rushes, we can begin to understand the immense, irreversible, multi-faceted change that all this has brought to our cities.

One part of the digital revolution's permanent legacy is a mostly invisible telecommunication infrastructure that efficiently connects just about every inhabited place on the face of the earth to every other. Its visible complement is an enormous and growing collection of electronic instruments of displacement distributed throughout the human habitat—instruments of spatial displacement through remote connection, and of temporal displacement through recording and replay. These instruments link the new global infrastructure to particular places and human activities. They embed the virtual in the physical, and weave it seamlessly into daily urban life.

The smallest and now most numerous of them are the ones that fit in your pocket—mobile telephones, Blackberries, iPods, digital cameras and video cameras, video game players, GPS guidance systems, and other more specialized little boxes of electronics. Since pocket real estate is limited, and the miniaturization of electronics shows little sign of slowing down, boxes that were initially separate keep fusing to form new combinations. Telephones, for example, have merged with digital cameras and Web browsers, and are now acquiring audio and video recording and replay capability. Furthermore, with the imperialism that we have come to expect from the digital, these finger-friendly boxes have inexorably been virtualizing and taking over the functions of former occupants of pocket space—notebooks, address books, diaries, wallets, identity cards, and key chains.

Miniaturized instruments of displacement have become extensions of our mobile bodies. They can be used in sedentary mode, while walking or running, or even (at some peril) while driving. They scramble familiar spatial categories by extending the range of activities that an individual can engage in anywhere, at any time, and they enable new forms of social coordination and control by providing continuous accessibility, tracking, and verification of identity. You can spontaneously arrange an assignation on your mobile telephone, navigate electronically to it, and take a picture when you get there, but you will also leave traces in cyberspace as you do so.

At the next step up in scale are the instruments that you can carry in your briefcase or backpack. They temporarily occupy desktops, tabletops, laptops, aircraft tray tables, hotel rooms, and lounges, and have redefined the ergonomic, power supply, and network access requirements of furniture and spaces. Like pocket devices, they have sucked surrounding functions into screen space—first those of old-fashioned desktop items, which immediately reappeared as virtual documents, folders, trashcans, clocks, calendars, and other now-familiar graphical user interface icons. They have multiplied on-screen icons in the process of repeatedly conquering new functional frontiers and ruthlessly exterminating the indigenous artifacts that had held sway before. This process has overlaid the (mostly) ancient, sedentary activities of the reader, writer, viewer, listener, scholar, librarian, file clerk, and accountant onto architectural settings that had not previously encompassed them. A café table becomes a place for a student to write a term paper, and an aircraft seat a place for a salesperson to edit a PowerPoint presentation.

At larger scale still, instruments of displacement are built into the architecture. As solid-state displays have supplanted cathode ray tubes, fat boxes have shrunk to slim slabs that can either be propped up on pedestals (like canvases on easels) or hung on walls to provide programmable signage, news and entertainment, and advertising. Even more extended display surfaces now slip their frames to spread across entire walls, as on the façades fronting Times Square, or ceilings, as on the canopy covering Fremont Street in Las Vegas. Here they transfer the decorative and iconographic functions of architecture to screen space, prompting Robert Venturi to enthuse, in a recent essay: "*Viva* the façade as computer screen! *Viva* façades not reflecting light but emanating light—the building as a digital sparkling source of information, not as an abstract glowing source of light! . . . *Viva* iconography—not carved in stone for eternity but digitally changing for *now*, so that the inherently dangerous fascist propaganda, for instance, can be temporarily, not eternally, proclaimed!"

At the very largest scale, instruments of displacement occupy the subject's entire sensory field to create an immersive experience. Everything becomes screen space. Movie theaters first approximated this condition. Then the pioneers of computer graphics figured out that they could get an even more powerful effect, in a smaller space and with less material and energy, by moving the components as close as possible to the relevant organs—position-sensitive displays right up against eyeballs, speakers clamped on the ears, a microphone at the mouth, and gesture-sensing force-feedback devices in the hands—so that a virtual environment completely masked the subject's physical surroundings. Immersive virtual reality and augmented reality systems were all the rage for a while, like flared pants or *Wired* magazine, and inspired a whole subgenre of cyberpunk fiction, but they eventually turned out to have fairly limited, specialized uses in simulation and entertainment.

The wholesale transfer of functionality and attention to screen space, where the distant and the past are continuously available, is the lasting legacy of the digital revolution. And this has produced a profound transformation of subjectivity. Like the instruments of paper-based reading, writing, and text storage and distribution before them, electronic instruments of displacement have taken us another step further away from the Edenic condition of living entirely in the here and now, and allow *homo electronicus* endless shifts of attention and engagement throughout the reaches of space and time.

For many of us, the moment we heard about the Bay of Bengal tsunami will lodge in memory like the moment we heard that JFK had been shot. The tsunami will be remembered not only as a terrible natural disaster, but also for its stark and powerful demonstration of the ethical implications of Marshall McLuhan's term "global village."

In November 1963, I happened to be walking down Bourke Street in Melbourne when I heard the newsboys yelling "Extra!" By chance, I was again near Melbourne, looking out over the stormy Southern Ocean—as vivid a scene as one could wish for of the raging, threatening sea—when the first bulletins telling of a tragedy in Sumatra came in over the Internet. Before long, the Yahoo, CNN, and BBC news Websites were giving details. Then television news footage began to appear from around the Indian Ocean. Within a few hours, bloggers had begun to post photographs and eyewitness accounts. Next morning's newspaper had page after page of terrifying reports, pictures of the smashed main street of Phuket, and before-and-after satellite photographs of Banda Aceh. When I strolled downtown to run a few errands, there was already a table, with a volunteer collecting relief donations, set up outside the local pub.

After a while, my mind sought some relief from all this and it leapt to a famous tamer of the sea, the great navigator Mathew Flinders. Two centuries ago, he had brilliantly charted the waters before me, and then set sail for home across the Indian Ocean. Having no way of knowing that hostilities had been renewed between England and France, he put in at the French naval base in Mauritius—where, to his surprise and fury, he was detained as a security threat for six years. It was a long time before anyone in Australia or London heard of his plight. In those days, the Indian Ocean was fringed with the colonies of competing empires, and news traveled very slowly among them and back to the European capitals.

I thought, then, of how things had changed by the time of the great explosion of Krakatoa in 1883. At the southern tip of Sumatra, it wasn't very far from Banda Aceh, and it produced a similar tsunami—one that destroyed hundreds of towns and killed tens of thousands of people around the Sunda Strait. But by this point, the colonies had been linked by submarine cables. A nearby Lloyd's agent took advantage of them to telegraph his office in London within minutes. *The Times* quickly ran a story, and Reuter's news agency peddled it around the world. As Simon Winchester remarked in his book *Krakatoa*, this signaled the emergence of the global village. It was the first story ever "about a truly enormous natural event that was both *about* the world and told *to* the world."

Of course, distant readers of the news could not actually *do* much for the victims of Krakatoa, and that probably didn't greatly worry them. Before the condition that we now know as globalization fully emerged, it was possible to argue that moral obligation to one's fellow human beings diminished rapidly with distance. (The Victorian moral philosopher Henry Sidgwick, for one, cogently did so in his influential *Methods of Ethics*.) Parents, spouses, and children were likely to be very close at hand—very possibly in the same house. Other relatives, neighbors, and friends were probably in the same town. Fellow countrymen formed a wider geographic circle, and the subjects of an empire a more extended circle still. Communities were place-based, and within them the sense of collective enterprise and mutual obligation tempered self-interest. But webs of social interaction attenuated as they spread out from their centers, so it seemed reasonable enough to assume that obligation did as well. You had many ethical obligations to those with whom you interacted intensely, over extended periods, but fewer to those with whom your interactions were limited or blocked by the impedance of distance. Distant disasters, therefore, did not demand the same sort of response as those in your own back yard—and such response would not have been practical anyway.

During the twentieth century, the development of fast sea and air transportation, combined with increasingly sophisticated telecommunications, progressively dismantled this neat geographic hierarchy. As a result, when we first heard of the tsunami, many of us thought immediately of relatives, friends, and colleagues who could have been in its path. Perhaps some of them were holidaying at the many resorts scattered throughout the area. Perhaps some were there on business. There were urgent phone calls and emails to try to track them down. The International Red Cross FamilyLinks Website, set up "to help those separated by conflict or disaster to find information about their loved ones in order to restore contact," crashed under a deluge of access requests. Individuals posted photographs of missing relatives and pleas for information on their personal Websites—electronic versions of the heartbreaking fliers that had been pinned up around Manhattan in the wake of 9/11. Volunteers photographed the dead and injured in Phuket's hospitals and emergency centers, posted them online on a site called Peoplematch, and ran face recognition software to match them with uploaded pictures of missing friends and relatives. The technologies of biometric security systems, and even of Internet dating, suddenly found urgent new uses.

Two weeks after the disaster, around 9,000 foreign tourists from dozens of countries were dead, missing, or unaccounted for. But it was not only through the traveling elite of the developed world that the human effects were propagated. Even more significantly, vast migrations of Indians, Indonesians, Sri Lankans, and Thais had established long-distance ties of family and friendship to many of the hundreds of thousands of local victims. And hundreds of very poor Burmese migrant workers died in Thailand. The impact extended across ethnic, religious, and socio-economic lines, and it was truly global.

The systems of global communication and mobilization that have enabled these extended human linkages grew from the efforts of pioneers like Mathew Flinders. They were put in place primarily to support a global economic system and global capacity for military action. They can be hijacked, as the last decade has shown us, for purposes of global terrorism. But they have also created the possibility of delivering supplies and relief workers quickly to disaster sites, and of enabling rebuilding efforts that draw upon the resources of the entire world. They create an expectation of response from the developed world—grudgingly acknowledged, at the very least, in the recognition that the conditions cannot be allowed to "breed terrorism." And they eliminate any remaining excuse for inaction.

Only time will tell how effective the international response will be, but so far the signs are heartening. If Krakatoa marked the violent birth of the global village, we can hope that the Bay of Bengal tsunami will be recorded in history as the moment at which the global village matured into a true community of mutual obligation and care.

Christo and Jeanne-Claude's The Gates—installed in New York's Central Park for two weeks—consists of seven thousand brightly colored steel, plastic, and fabric objects parked along the pathways that meander through the vast rectangle. In homage to the great Marcel Duchamp, I hereby declare that the rest of Manhattan is an even larger, more dynamic, more participatory public art project entitled The Cars.

The effect of The Gates is much like that of marking up a familiar text with a highlighter. Some things unexpectedly pop out at you. Previously prominent landmarks, like the statue of Daniel Webster, recede into the background. Disconcertingly, the structural unity of Frederick Law Olmsted and Calvert Vaux's great composition disappears and a vivid new pattern appears in its place. The old way of seeing the park will be back when The Gates come down, but memories of a brief and powerful makeover will remain. When you first catch sight of the orange fabric flapping in the wind, you know that you will henceforth read the landscape against the recollection of its transfiguration.

The only other thing so famously orange in New York these days is the remarkable coifed hair of Donald Trump—developer of glitzy-tacky apartment towers, star of *The Apprentice*, and contender with Harvard's Larry Summers for the title of America's most obnoxious boss. For some reason, the artists insist that the color of their enormous installation is actually saffron—the pure and delicate hue of water infused with the precious stigmata of the saffron crocus, of risotto Milanese, and of Buddhist robes—but nobody is buying that. Instead, the relentlessly repeated archways evoke safety rainwear, Fanta, the plastic mesh that surrounds excavations in New York's streets, the spray paint that tells repair crews where to dig up the pavement, and (in my neighborhood, at least) municipal garbage trucks. The color is clearly a product of precisely controlled industrial chemistry rather than of nature, but it is carefully calibrated to contrast with the seasonal, nuanced grays of the rocks, the leafless trees, the icy lakes, and the sky. While the mobile phone companies Orange and easyMobile fight in the courts about the right to use similar shades as signatures in their advertising, *this* precise variant will be Christo's amber forever.

It is hard to tell whether the artists are buying in, selling out, or sending up—which has the advantage of disconcerting the New York art crowd, who like to know where they stand on such matters. You can take the whole thing as a knowing satire on capitalist culture's veneration of the art of the deal. It was cleverly financed—to the tune of $20 million—through the sale of Christo's drawings, and enabled through an agreement hammered out with New York's businessman mayor. Like Henry

Ford, the artists drove the cost down through standardization and mass production. (You can have any color you want, so long as it's orange.) Nonetheless, it was a nice order for the fabric manufacturers and plastic and steel fabricators to get. Christo and Jeanne-Claude organized an army of helpers, and ran an impeccably orchestrated publicity campaign. They created a midwinter cash cow for the city, drawing thousands of visitors and filling up hotel rooms and restaurants. The materials, of course, will be recycled. Surely it was all tongue-in-cheek? Then again, they might simply have been doing what they needed to do to complete the project. Their deadpan demeanor gave nothing away.

The likes of the Disney Corporation know how to make money out of expensively produced art, and few complain that it is a waste or a confidence trick when they build huge sets for the sake of a single shot and end up sinking tens of millions of dollars into a motion picture. But their business model depends upon the public's well-established willingness to pay for representation and narrative, whereas Christo and Jeanne-Claude seem to have invented a new model to support the modernist practice of non-narrative abstraction. Insofar as their work is *about* anything, it is about being very, very orange on a very large scale, yet it did somehow get paid for. Furthermore, it did not depend on ticket sales, or generate an opening weekend gross for *Variety* to report; admission to Central Park remains free. If you are curious enough to follow the money, you quickly appreciate the paradox of generating the necessary cash flow from realistic representations of a non-representational work that did not yet exist—that is, Christo's high-class architectural renderings of the project. You hear visitors trying to figure out this shell game, and muttering that somebody must be getting fleeced, somewhere.

Architects can look to it as an example of actually existing frozen music. The repetition of the units lays down an insistent beat, like that of a rapper. Within this framework, the wind improvises endlessly varying figures that emerge, progress, and then die away. (This recalls the Running Fence project in California, in 1976, but here the wind figures have a rhythm rather than a sinuous flow.) The continually changing light, together with the varied angles of the fabric to the sun, creates fluctuating ranges of intensities against the constancy of a fixed hue—producing, on occasion, the dramatic chiaroscuro of backlit fabric deep within the shadows. There is a feeling of frenetic compression where gates crowd together at the southern end of the park, near Columbus Circle, then a meandering movement north—circling around Sheep Meadow, Strawberry Fields, and The Ramble—accompanied by gradual attenuation into lonely strings of fabric across a frozen and mostly empty landscape. The most beautiful moment comes on sunny mornings, when you catch sight of a distant line of orange creating a glow among the bare trees across the lake, with the formidable apartment towers of Central Park West rising in the background.

"Gates" is a term that suggests a function as well as a form, and indeed the arched units seem directly modeled on the sequences of reddish orange torii gates found at Shinto shrines such as the Fushimi Inari in Kyoto. Here, though, the form of the gate is emptied of any real function and surreally multiplied. Ultimately, Christo and Jeanne-Claude have slyly transferred to the center of Manhattan a motif characteristic of the industrial era's most spooky and desolate urban margins—the patch of ground that has been invaded by mass production's post-functional detritus. The Gates powerfully connects the capital of capitalism to a global system of car-wreckers' yards on the outskirts of town, used tire dumps, the ship graveyards of Chittagong, the mothballed airplanes lined up in the Mojave Desert, the heaps of old computer monitors, circuit boards, and other e-junk being recycled in the miserable Chinese city of Guiyu, and those neglected trees filled with windblown plastic bags that some unknown poet has likened to witches' knickers.

Oscar Wilde aside, going to jail can be a great career move for a writer. Nobody would remember Richard Lovelace if not for his jingling jailhouse lines, "Stone walls do not a prison make, nor iron bars a cage." Look what it did for the Marquis de Sade. And where would the theory of hegemony be without Gramsci's *Prison Notebooks*? So I'm hoping that Martha Stewart has been scribbling in the slammer. She's a smart, tough, and articulate woman, and would certainly provide us with a more acutely observed take on white-collar prison living than, say, Jeffrey Archer, or the smarmy kleptocrats of Enron and WorldCom. I'd look forward to *Martha Stewart Living Inside*, or *The 120 Days of Bad Food*. Unfortunately, her brand management consultants will probably advise against it.

Stewart's cell in West Virginia wasn't like the dungeon in Vincennes where the wicked Marquis—getting horrid meals shoved at him through the bars, raging at the mother-in-law who had put him there, and bored out of his mind—began to document the lifestyle that he had devoted himself to demonstrating, and that would eventually be branded with his name.

(I don't think Martha has ever acknowledged how much her business model owes to the Marquis. Harvard Business School case writers please note.) In fact, the Alderson Federal Prison Camp for women, where she served five months, is widely known as Camp Cupcake. The living quarters don't look much worse than most college dorms, and there are no razor wire fences or armed guards. The campus-like facility functions as a virtual prison where inmates are not physically prevented from stepping outside its boundaries, but face heavy fines and additional jail time if they do. This is a common enough arrangement in Sweden, but it tends to drop jaws in a country that spends far more on constructing high-security prisons than on public housing. As de Sade understood perfectly though, razor wire does not a prison make. The essence of incarceration is not the hardware of confinement but the state of mind induced by continual surveillance and the calibrated expression of control.

Post-Cupcake, the domestic diva is doing five more months in a wireless electronic version of the same thing. She is required to wear an ankle bracelet that controls her movements—turning her big house into a Big House. Unlike the popular canine collar implementation of this cute notion, it does not give her an electric shock if she takes a step too far, but simply transmits an alert to her jailers if she strays or shucks it. And she is no doubt thankful that it is marginally more chic, in an edgy sort of way, than a carceral choker.

This device has been with us for a while. Like the iPod that substitutes for a theater and the laptop computer that substitutes for an office, it replaces a traditional building type by overlaying the functions of that type on the urban environment in general. And like that other triumph of wireless portable electronics, the cellular telephone, it has gradually evolved to a smaller and more elegant form factor. It is unlikely to become a must-have fashion item, though—except, maybe, with the Marquis-*manqué* leather-and-bondage crowd. An obvious part of the point is humiliation, while providing endless reminders of transgression, through the exhibition of a symbolically violated body. In other words, it continues the grand old tradition of the scarlet letter on the forehead, the cuffed perp walk, and chopping off the hands of thieves. Martha Stewart is one of the most photographed people on the planet, and it's her job to display her line of accessories, but it's safe to say that we won't be seeing any ankle shots in the near future.

Imagine, though, that the bracelet came in silver, gold, platinum, and corporate versions, and was relentlessly promoted as a prestige item that allowed you to charge purchases, open locked doors, pay your turnpike tolls, make telephone calls, or perform any of the myriad tasks that we now assign to plastic cards, transponders in automobiles, RFID tags, and keychain and pocket electronic devices. Maybe it would be small enough to wear as a ring, or for Motorola to build into wristwatches and telephones. It would be more convenient, and it would simply make explicit the bargain that these proliferating devices already present to us. You can have the convenience and the status, provided that you accept the continuous construction of a detailed electronic trace of your movements and actions. Unlike Martha Stewart, you are not compelled to check in to the virtual prison; you are simply seduced, by the sort of marketing that she is so adept at, into doing it voluntarily.

For most of us, this electronically maintained virtual prison still seems more like Camp Cupcake than Alcatraz. One reason is that the varied and scattered electronic traces that we create are not routinely pulled together to create detailed pictures of our daily lives. But this is technically feasible, and it is precisely the sort of capability that some of the scarier intelligence agencies have been creating, and demanding the legal right to use, in the post-9/11 era that makes "everything different." The electronic watchtowers are going up. And so are the boundaries and checkpoints as this surveillance enables watch lists at airport security gates and other electronically serviced sites of control. Stone walls are an expensive way to make a prison now, and places like Guantanomo Bay tend to rebound and discredit their originators, but through the miracles of digital networking and Moore's Law, jailers and would-be jailers now have other means.

But electronic technology does not autonomously produce virtual prisons, any more than the technology of stone construction creates traditional prisons. Prisons, of course, result from the appropriation and deployment of available technologies to serve legal and political ends. In the aftermath of 9/11, the Italian philosopher Giorgio Agamben put a new spin on this point by refusing to be photographed and fingerprinted on entry to the United States, and canceling plans to teach a course at New York University. He was not willing, he announced in *Le Monde* (10 January, 2004) to wear the electronically constructed "bio-political tattoo." The American press reported this as the hysterical reaction of an eccentric academic. But students of political philosophy were reminded of his erudite and influential texts distinguishing between bare biological existence and the ethically guided political life of citizens, on the legitimacy of claims to sovereign power, and on the normalization of states of exception. And they recalled, with sudden shudders, his closely reasoned conclusion that the West's political paradigm was no longer the city state but the concentration camp, no longer Athens but Auschwitz.

Carriage Return

I was born in a lonely flyspeck on the absurdly empty map of the Australian interior. When I eventually took an interest in such things, I discovered that Mark Twain had once passed through there, and had written in *Following the Equator*: "Horsham sits in a plain which is as level as the floor—one of those famous dead levels which Australian books describe so often; gray, bare, somber, melancholy, baked, cracked, in the tedious long droughts, but a horizonless ocean of vivid green grass the day after a rain. A country town, peaceful, reposeful, inviting, full of snug houses, with garden plots, and plenty of shrubbery and flowers."

We moved away when I was very small, but I still remember the river—arched over with red gums, and loud with the sound of magpies, kookaburras, and the occasional screech of a cockatoo. You could stand on the bridge and drop stones to plonk into the muddy water. There was a broad main street, with shop verandahs and angle parking for the few cars. The baker, the milkman, and the iceman delivered from horse-drawn carts. Across the Natimuk Road were dry, grassy paddocks, and my dad always carried a big stick for the snakes when we walked there. Old Baldy Anderson (though nobody called him that to his face) ran the pub.

Every evening, the express train from Melbourne came thundering into town—passing through, and barely pausing, on its way to Adelaide. You could hear the whistle blowing—with urgently increasing intensity, then a mournful, gorgeous Doppler shift—from miles away across the starlit plains. The locomotive was a magnificent smoking, hissing, clacking monster sporting a glowing firebox, a tender heaped with filthy coal, and huge, shiny wheels. It was my earliest intimation of the technological sublime.

Throughout my bush childhood, the trains served as mobile metonyms for a wider world. In the slang of the day, the sprawling coastal cities were "the big smoke," and the steam engines were the fleeting local bearers of that emblematic attribute. They puffed great clouds of it up into the otherwise perfect hemisphere of clear blue sky, and left long plumes trailing across the flat horizon—matched, occasionally, by the dust plumes from cars speeding along dirt roads. When you entered a tunnel on the train, you had to leap up to close all the windows; otherwise, your compartment filled instantly with choking soot.

Each warmly lit carriage interior was a synecdoche of urbanity—an encapsulated, displaced fragment of the mysterious life that was lived at the end of the line. The passengers dressed differently from the locals, and they talked of unfamiliar things. They carried with them the Melbourne newspapers—the sober and serious broadsheet the *Age*, the racy *Sun* and *Argus*, the evening *Herald*, the *Weekly Times* (printed, for some reason, on pink paper), and the utterly scandalous tabloid *Truth*. News was scarce in the bush, in the days before portable radios and casual long-distance calls, so fresh papers were eagerly awaited; passengers would sometimes toss them out to the railway workers who stood leaning on their shovels as a train groaned slowly by, much as they might offer a smoke to a stranger, or slip some flour and tea to a swagman at the door.

The passenger compartments were beautifully crafted in polished wood, overstuffed leather, screwed brass and chrome fittings, frosted glass with railway insignia, heavy sliding doors that closed with a satisfying thump, and little enamel notices enumerating prohibitions—spitting, smoking in the wrong places, frivolously pulling the emergency brake chain, and flushing the toilet while the train was stopped at a station. They were meticulously equipped with hooks for the broad-brimmed hats that all the men wore, ashtrays for the heaped remnants of cigarettes (some old-timers, I observed with amazement, could casually roll their next smokes with one hand while stubbing out the last with the other), overhead racks for suitcases, and chemical foot warmers that you would take out from under the seats and shake to activate. And they were wondrous cabinets of curiosities, with friezes of large, sepia photographs over the seats—each one depicting a ferny gully, a gravel track lined by huge eucalyptus trees, a mountain lookout, a wild patch of coast, or some other picturesque scene from the extensive territory served by the Victorian Railways. When I was a little older, and my family had picked up and moved to the shores of the Southern Ocean, the Jubilee Train came to town—a celebration of the fiftieth anniversary of the federation of the former colonies and formation of the Australian nation—and it overflowed with the vast, varied, and unruly world condensed into a collection of mementos and souvenirs. I saw famous gold nuggets, the bullet-dented armor of the outlaw Ned Kelly, creepy remnants of the cruel convict era, stuffed birds and animals, diving helmets, feathery coral and giant clams from far-away Queensland, miscellaneous mineral specimens, and yellowing old documents.

It was on a train, long before I was reluctantly dragged off to school, that I first realized I could read. With my nose up against the window, I began to decipher the signs advertising

Bushell's Tea, the mileage markers that crept by, and the names of the stations where we creaked to successive stops—words in memorable sequence, the beginnings of narrative. I quickly found that the made-up narratives of books vanquished the boring hours as we crept across the plains. It wasn't long before I ran through the meager supply of kids' books, and moved on to the volumes of Henry Lawson that I had discovered at home. Lawson, to my gratified astonishment, wrote not of the Old Country and the Empire, nor of exotic American adventure, but of the people and places I *knew*. He was the bard of the bush. I loved the deadpan desolation of his great stories "The Drover's Wife" and "The Union Buries Its Dead." I could readily have believed that his famous character Mitchell the bushman, arriving with battered swag and old cattle-dog at Sydney's Redfern railway station, was a long-lost uncle. I was stirred by his angry anthem of the underdog, "Faces in the Street." And sometimes it seemed that he was sitting beside me, gazing out into the shimmering distance:

By homestead, hut, and shearing-shed,
By railroad, coach, and track—
By lonely graves of our brave dead,
Up-Country, and Out-Back:
To where 'neath glorious clustered stars
The dreamy plains expand—
My home lies wide, a thousand miles
In the Never-Never Land.

It didn't matter that he had some patch of Western Queensland in mind when he wrote those lines. It didn't matter that he had died, drunk and penniless on the streets of Sydney, decades ago. I knew exactly what he meant. The power of his words, magically locking on to the landscape before me, made him vividly present.

When I was learning to write schoolboy essays of my own, perched at a wooden desk with porcelain inkwell and steel-nibbed pen, I often thought of sentences as trains. You could shunt the words around, like rolling stock on a siding, until you got them in exactly the right order. Like empty boxcars, they could carry the freight of simile and metaphor. And verbs, surely, were locomotives. Put them up front for snappy imperatives. Multiply, mass, and combine them for extra power. Keep it short. On the other hand, if the mood took you, and you wanted to construct a long, slow, freight-train of a sentence, with reflective asides in the manner of writers like Joseph Furphy, you could just let a few scattered verbs help it along from somewhere in the middle. Or, for a different effect, they might follow, pushing. When I memorized and recited poetry from the *School Reader*—mostly jingling ballads, like "The Wreck of the Hesperus" and "The Man from Snowy River," the rhythms of the rails were always on my mind. Eventually, I got to read Pope on poetry, and realized he was right: the sound must seem an echo of the sense.

As the years went by, and I made myself into an architect and urbanist, I began to understand that objects, narratives, memories, and space are woven into a complex, expanding web—each fragment of which gives meaning to all the others. For me, it was a web that grew from a quiet, isolated place on the banks of the Wimmera River.

It is more than half a century, now, since I left that little town. A decade or so later, when I had the chance to attend

Melbourne University, I fled the bush forever and have since lived my life among the world's great cities. But the sight of an express train still evokes the other end of the line. Now it recovers the memory of a spreading, aromatic peppercorn tree, a corrugated iron roof that was too hot to touch when you climbed up to retrieve a ball, the sudden smell of raindrops in the dust, and a small, curious child—walking with his impossibly young and beautiful parents along a silent, sunburned street.

Acknowledgments

"Do We Still Need Skyscrapers?" originally appeared in *Scientific American*, December 1997, pp. 112–113, and is reproduced with permission. The remainder of the texts in "Text and the City" originally appeared as monthly columns in the *Royal Institute of British Architects Journal* from February 2003 to May 2005. In some cases the titles differ, and there are some minor variations in the texts due to the differing conventions of periodical and book publication, but the pieces are essentially as they originally appeared. I wish to thank my editors at *RIBA J*, Naomi Stungo and Amanda Baillieu, for their enthusiastic support of the column and their frequent helpful suggestions. "Carriage Return" was originally written for Sherry Turkle's *Evocative Objects* project at MIT.

Index